Life, Death,
and Archaeology at
Fort Blue Mounds

Life, Death, and Archaeology at

FORT BLUE MOUNDS

A Settlers' Fortification of the Black Hawk War

Robert A. Birmingham

Wisconsin Historical Society Press

Published by the Wisconsin Historical Society Press
Publishers since 1855

© 2012 by the State Historical Society of Wisconsin

Publication of this book was made possible in part by a grant from the D.C. Everest fellowship fund.

wisconsin**history**.org

Photos and illustrations are from the author unless otherwise specified.

Photographs identified with WHi or WHS are from the Society's collections; address requests to reproduce these photos to the Visual Materials Archivist at the Wisconsin Historical Society, 816 State Street, Madison, WI 53706.

Cover art from the Friends of the Military Ridge Trail Interpretive Center Mural in Ridgeway, Wisconsin. Project artist: Ingrid Kallick; project historian: Tom McKay. Funded by a grant from the Wisconsin Humanities Council. Photo by Mark Fay.

Printed in the United States of America

Designed by Diana Boger

16 15 14 13 12   1 2 3 4 5

Library of Congress Cataloging-in-Publication Data

Birmingham, Robert A.

  Life, death, and archaeology at Fort Blue Mounds : a settlers' fortification of the Black Hawk War / Robert A. Birmingham.

    p. cm.

  Includes bibliographical references and index.

  ISBN 978-0-87020-492-0 (pbk. : alk. paper) 1. Fort Blue Mounds (Wis.) 2. Excavations (Archaeology)—Wisconsin)—Fort Blue Mounds. 3. Frontier and pioneer life)—Wisconsin)—Fort Blue Mounds. 4. Black Hawk War, 1832)—Antiquities. I. Title.

  F587.D3B57 2012

  977.5'83--dc23

                    2012018868

CONTENTS

≋ Acknowledgments ≋

Tʜɪs ʙᴏᴏᴋ ᴛᴇʟʟs the dramatic story of Fort Blue Mounds during the Black Hawk War, describes the search for and discovery of its remains, and offers insights as to what the historical and archeological research conveys about life during the war and on the frontier at the time. The larger story of the Black Hawk War is nearly incomprehensible to us today since it is far removed in time, circumstance, and worldviews. The past is a foreign country, as once noted by British novelist L. P. Hartley. It is now difficult for us to put ourselves in the place of those Indian people risking their lives against all odds to retain their lands and culture; or in the place of those who would deprive an entire people of their homes and their very lives in order to secure their own place in a new nation; or in the place of frightened settlers who sought only to begin new, productive lives for themselves and their children, facing the great challenges each day brought. However, smaller stories like those of the Blue Mounds community offer us a more intimate journey into the foreign land of the past as we're guided by the eyes and hands of those who lived there. The archaeological research even provided participants with an opportunity to literally touch history.

I am grateful to the many volunteers who devoted weekends to excavating the site through heat, cold, rain, and worms. I enjoyed their company thoroughly, and they performed to the high standards of professional archaeology. These are Ben Anderson, Linda Anderson, Neil Anderson, Amy Bandle, Dave Beard, Brian Birger, Nancy Birmingham, Barbara Bray, Eileen Carlson, Barbara Chattergee, Mik Derks, Bruce and Wesley Ellerson, Jane and Virgina Evans, Harvey Fedler, Tom Fey, Bill Figi, Ellen Figi, Nora Figi, Bruce Fischer and family, Adam Fleming, Terry Genske, Stephen Gilbert, Richard Gill, Bob Halseth, Colleen Hermans, Angela Horn, Gary Howards and family, the Hull family, Jan Jensen, Allan Korbitz, Craig Malven, Norm Meimholz, Jerry Minnich, Joe Monarski, Jessica Nowicki, Rebecca Perkins, Helene Pohl, Al Schmidt, Jennifer Scot, Steve Steigerwald, Tom Waddell, Bill Wamback, Pat Wirtz, Harley Young, Bob Zimmerman, and Boy Scout Troop 34 of Madison.

Henry Eckel, Jessy Straubhaar, and Reini Straubhaar—owners of surrounding lands—graciously allowed access to the site and helped the project in many material ways. Valonne Eckel, who lives in a house adjacent to the site, put up with a yard full of vehicles during many summer weekends and also donated artifacts she found as a child on the fort site. Full-time and part-time Wisconsin Historical Society archaeology staff, mainly students at the time—William Gartner (PhD, University of Wisconsin–Madison, 2003); John Hodgson and Tom Ritzenthaler (University of Wisconsin–Madison); John Orie (Oneida Nation); and Amy Rosebrough and Robert Simpkins (PhDs, University of Wisconsin–Madison, 2010)—assisted in various ways in excavation, research, and analysis. My son, Kevin Birmingham, assisted me with some of the photography and in many other ways.

Steve Kuehn, now of the Illinois Transportation Archaeology Program, analyzed animal bone recovered during the excavation while working for the Wisconsin Historical Society Museum Archaeology Program. Bob Braun of the Old Lead Mine Region Historical Society and Bob Mazrim of the Illinois Transportation Archaeology Program shared their expertise on period artifacts and history. After I retired from the Wisconsin Historical Society in 2004, the institution provided me with access to the collections and extended many professional courtesies.

Doing archaeology and writing history offer many opportunities for error, and I alone take responsibility for any errors in fact or interpretation that may have crept into this book.

∽ PREFACE ∽

Dᴜʀɪɴɢ ᴛʜᴇ Bʟᴀᴄᴋ Hᴀᴡᴋ Wᴀʀ ᴏғ 1832, settlers of Blue Mounds in Michigan Territory, now the state of Wisconsin, formed a volunteer militia, built a fort, and lived there for nearly three months while enduring anxiety, deprivations, and violent death. The conflict began when the Sauk warrior leader Black Hawk crossed the Mississippi River from what is now Iowa with a band of approximately 1,100 men, women, and children to continue life on ancestral lands in Illinois that had been claimed by the United States government through a controversial treaty. Federal troops and state and territorial volunteer militia tried to stop the defiant Black Hawk and return his people to the land they had been removed to west of the Mississippi. Blocked from resettling, the Indian band moved northward, chased by the military and engaging in short but deadly skirmishes. War parties from Black Hawk's band and some warriors from other tribes launched attacks on settlers and settlements, creating panic throughout the Upper Midwest.

Messages and rumors concerning the northward movement of Black Hawk's band, along with deadly encounters and attacks, had reached the small lead-mining community of Blue Mounds, located thirty miles west of the present-day state capital of Madison. The settlers hastily erected a fort in May 1832, one of at least seventy-eight temporary fortifications built by the panicked white population in southwestern Wisconsin, Illinois, and beyond.

The frontier settlers of Blue Mounds—mostly lead miners—feared the worst, and, indeed, the occupants of the fort found themselves engulfed by the conflict. Because of its strategic location relative to Black Hawk's movements, the fort served as a center for militia and US Army activities.

In 1910 descendants of Blue Mounds settlers deeded the land around the remains of the fort to the Wisconsin Historical Society, which subsequently erected a small historical maker to tell the story of the important Black Hawk War site.

In 1991 a modern group of volunteers converged on the site of Fort Blue Mounds to relocate and document its remains. Land development was creeping westward from the suburbs of Madison toward the modern village of Blue Mounds. Subdivisions had already begun to pop up within eyesight of the hill where the fort had once stood, and it became clear that development could soon impinge on the fort site. The precise location of the fort was unclear, however, and this needed to be determined if this part of our history was to be preserved.

Dedication of the historical marker at the site of Fort Blue Mounds in 1921

WHi Image ID 79795

As Wisconsin state archaeologist at the time, I had the responsibility of locating and preserving important archaeological sites such as Fort Blue Mounds. In this case, the site was located on land owned by the Wisconsin Historical Society, my employer, so the motivation was even greater. The Black Hawk War was also of great interest to me personally. I had crossed Black Hawk's trail throughout my professional life. As a new graduate student at the University of Wisconsin–Milwaukee in the mid-1970s, I had been assigned an archaeological survey of the Illinois Black Hawk country— the lands along the Rock River, extending from the Wisconsin border to the confluence the Rock and Mississippi Rivers in Illinois, that had been the site of Black Hawk's home village, Saukenuk. At one point, our archaeological team looked for ancient artifacts under the immense Lorado Taft concrete sculpture of a generic Native American man at Lowden-Miller State Park near Oregon, Illinois, often assumed to be Black Hawk by the public. At Rock Island, Ferrel Anderson, head of the Quad Cities Archaeological Society at the time, took me on tour of what had once been Saukenuk but was now covered by the city of Rock Island. I remember being perplexed that such an important place had not been preserved or commemorated, and I hoped that one day I could do something about such matters.

That opportunity presented itself when I later joined the Wisconsin Historical Society's Historic Preservation division as an archaeologist. In 1989, the year I was appointed Wisconsin state archaeologist, local residents brought it to my attention that the privately owned site of the Wisconsin Heights battlefield was threatened with development. Wisconsin Heights was the site of a short but intense battle on July 21, 1832, between militia and Indian warriors defending Black Hawk's band. Coincidentally, the state of Wisconsin had just implemented the Lower Wisconsin Riverway Program, headed by Dave Gjestson of the Department of Natural Resources, for the purpose of preserving lands and scenic views along the river. Funds were available for the state to acquire important lands along the river. Dave proved not only receptive but quite enthusiastic about state purchase of the property, and it was quickly arranged through his leadership.

Dave went on to take a great personal interest in the battle site and the Black Hawk War. With help from volunteers, he restored the oak savanna and added interpretive signage at the site. He applied for and received a federal historic preservation grant, administered by the Wisconsin

Historical Society's Historic Preservation division, to undertake an archaeological survey and historical study. In 1994, Dave headed a Wisconsin Sesquicentennial project that led to the installation of sixteen new historical markers along Black Hawk's trail in the state and the creation of a driving tour map.

In 2001 Dave and I had the honor of coordinating a Wisconsin Historical Society–sponsored bus tour of Wisconsin Black Hawk War places to about forty descendants of Black Hawk and his band, the Sac and Fox Nation of Oklahoma. During a ceremony at the Wisconsin Heights battlefield, Sac and Fox officials presented the Wisconsin Historical Society with the nation's flag. At the site of the Bad Axe massacre, now a public recreation area, tribal members quietly put tobacco offerings in the Mississippi River in memory of their ancestors who were killed there. Dave and I also organized a well-attended 175th anniversary commemorative program of the Wisconsin Heights battle in 2007, which also featured representatives from the Sac and Fox Nation, as well as state and local officials.

It was in 1989 that I had learned, to my surprise, that the Wisconsin Historical Society owned property containing at least part of Fort Blue Mounds. With the help of the late Elizabeth Brigham Rooney, local historian and descendant of an early settler of Blue Mounds, I found the long-neglected historical marker in the middle of a cornfield on a high hill south of the modern community of Blue Mounds. But there were no visible signs of the fort, and the cement posts that had once marked the corners of the Wisconsin Historical Society site were broken and piled up in front of the marker. Back at the Wisconsin Historical Society, Associate Director Robert Thomasgard showed me the original document deeding the quarter-acre property to the state agency, but it proved of little value because it contained no external reference. The property description located the land only in relation to the remnants of the fort itself, and these once visible remnants had been erased by farming and time in the years since the deed was made. Further, historical sources described a large fortification—one much larger than the deeded acreage. Even if the boundaries of the quarter acre could be relocated, there still remained the question of what part of the fort was on the historical society's property and therefore preserved. Archaeological work would have to be done to determine these facts. It was time for the shovel and trowel!

More than seventy-five volunteers worked on the Fort Blue Mounds project over eight summer seasons. Many brought their families. One Boy Scout troop devoted time to learn more about archaeology and local history. To accommodate volunteer schedules, the work was done weekends, with an average of eight weekends spent each summer working on the project—although the schedule was many times affected by typically erratic Wisconsin weather. During one memorably wet summer, only a few days could be spent actually digging. Returning to the excavations later that season, volunteers busied themselves with the obnoxious task of clearing thousands of worms from the moist excavation pits that had been covered with black plastic.

Terry Genske, a land surveyor by profession, directed mapping of the site. Howard Houghton, a direct descendant of militia volunteer William Houghton, also came forward to help with his wife, Betty. William Houghton, a blacksmith from Saint Louis, had been assigned to Fort Blue Mounds and was later compensated for his service with some land in Indiana, where he was born and raised. Howard provided much information on his great-great-grandfather, and he was overjoyed by the prospect of finding objects that his ancestor might have used—or even made, as was the case with hand-wrought nails unearthed in some abundance. Harvey Fedler, in his eighties at the time, had attained much previous experience volunteering for archaeology projects in the southwestern United States. No one, even the professionals, could match his abilities to trowel clean and square floors in the excavation units. Longtime Fort Blue Mounds volunteer and television producer Mik Derks incorporated the excavations into an award-winning program that aired on Wisconsin Public Television.

Even accounting for the limited seasonal schedule, the work took longer than expected, not only because of the discovery of interesting and informative fort remains but because exaggerated accounts of the fort size in historical accounts sometimes sent the team chasing false leads. However, patience and persistence are the primary virtues in archaeological research and, in 2000, the last bit of evidence was unearthed.

While digging and screening, volunteers had discussed the Black Hawk War, and many went home to read everything they could on the subject, sharing information and insights during the dig. The project produced a number of people with unusual familiarity with this aspect of American history. Many used their experience and new expertise to assist the Wisconsin Historical Society with other archaeological projects. Several of the younger participants went on to professional jobs in archaeology, much enthused by the Blue Mounds experience.

Based on the archaeological and historical research, the boundaries of the Fort Blue Mounds site were again marked, thus ending a successful historic preservation story and paving the way for future research and public education projects at the fort site.

<small>FIGURE 1.1</small>

a) Black Hawk, b) Colonel Henry Dodge, by George Catlin, c) General Henry Atkinson

<small>a) From Thomas McKenney and James Hall, *History of the Indian Tribes of North America*, b) WHi Image ID 27177, c) Courtesy of Northern Illinois University</small>

1

Fort Blue Mounds
& the Black Hawk War

In the spring of 1832 a terrifying series of alarms spread like prairie fire throughout the lead-mining region of northwestern Illinois and the part of Michigan Territory that is now southwestern Wisconsin. A large Native American force led by the Sauk warrior chief Black Hawk was headed north in that direction with the intent of attacking and driving out settlers (Figure 1.1). In April, Illinois governor John Reynolds proclaimed that Indians had "assumed a hostile attitude" and "invaded that state."[1] A month later, following a deadly skirmish between Black Hawk's warriors and a company of the Illinois militia on the Rock River, Colonel Henry Dodge of the Michigan Territory militia sent a message to US Army General Henry Atkinson saying that he would draw in the lead-mining settlements and "get the inhabitants to fort themselves."[2]

Rumors of war had already reached the tiny mining settlement of Blue Mounds in what is now Dane County, Wisconsin, and work on a log fort was well underway when Reynolds sent his alarm. The miner settlers feared not only Black Hawk's forces but a general uprising of neighboring Ho-Chunk (then known as Winnebago) people. Tension between settlers and Native Americans had been building for some time in the region, leading to the

1827 activation of the Iowa County regiment of the Michigan Territory militia headed by Dodge, a prominent and powerful lead miner, and under the general command of federal military authorities.[3] The people of Blue Mounds had surely hoped to escape conflict, but they instead found themselves drawn into what has come to be called the Black Hawk War. Over the next three months attacks by Native Americans took three lives, and the fort itself became a center of military operations. Fort Blue Mounds would also become the scene of a famous and dramatic hostage release.

The Black Hawk conflict of 1832 wasn't really much of a war in the traditional sense. It may be best described as a long chase, punctuated by skirmishes and short attacks, ending in a horrific massacre of Black Hawk's band that embarrassed and disgraced the US Army and volunteer militia companies. The conflict took the lives of at least five hundred Native Americans due to starvation, illness, battles, and especially the final massacre, as well as the lives of seventy-seven army soldiers, militia, and settlers.[4] It was similar to, but more lethal than, a much later event during which Nez Perce leader Chief Joseph (who, like Black Hawk, was also opposed to an unfair treaty) and eight hundred Nez Perce people evaded the federal army for three months in 1877, moving through Oregon, Washington, Idaho, Wyoming, and Montana before being stopped during a battle with federal troops just short of Canada, where Chief Joseph and his band had sought safety.[5]

Much modern historical analysis has been devoted to investigating the complex causes of the Black Hawk conflict and exploring Black Hawk's own motivation for leading an enterprise that seemed doomed from start.[6] However, the conflict that ensued can be broadly and most simply viewed as the direct consequence of encroaching white settlement on lands already occupied by Native Americans, which began in earnest in the Midwest during the early nineteenth century. Black Hawk himself summed up the situation simply when speaking of the loss of his beautiful Rock River homeland with its villages and cornfields: "I fought for it."[7]

Prelude

The subject of many books, articles, publications, and even modern websites, the events comprising the Black Hawk War are well known. Black Hawk dictated his own account to newspaper editor John P. Patterson, who published at least the gist of it as *Life of Ma-ka-tai-me-she-kia-kiak or Black Hawk* in

1833, and hundreds of primary documents generated by the military and other officials during the conflict are preserved in the extraordinary three-volume set *The Black Hawk War 1831-1832*, published by the Illinois State Historical Library.[8]

The chain of events leading to the conflict began in 1804 when the United States pressured a delegation from the combined Sauk and Fox (Mesquakie) Nation into ceding all of the lands they claimed east of the Mississippi River—a total of fifty million acres. At that time they were living primarily along the Mississippi River between the Wisconsin River and the Des Moines River, although there were scattered settlements elsewhere (Figure 1.2). The 1804 treaty stipulated that the Sauk and Fox could live on ceded lands until the lands were surveyed and sold to white settlers.

Many Sauk and Fox opposed the treaty and this caused a great division in the tribe. Among those opposed was Black Hawk, who had been born and lived in the village of Saukenuk near the mouth of the Rock River in

FIGURE 1.2

Sauk and Fox Indians, in a period drawing by Karl Bodmer

WHi Image ID 4519

Illinois. By 1832 he had become a distinguished, though aging, warrior chief. He had developed an animosity toward Americans early in his life because of that treaty, and consequently fought with the British in the War of 1812. Thereafter, Black Hawk continued to ally himself to the British, even traveling to Canada to trade. His enmity toward the Americans greatly increased as settlers flooded into Illinois and his people were pressured off their lands and forced across the Mississippi into modern-day Iowa. "Perhaps the principal factor in Black Hawk's decision to defy American officials," wrote historian Roger Nichols, "was his long standing sense that they had continually dealt unfairly and dishonestly with the Sauk."[9] Black Hawk had received an ancestral sacred bundle, or medicine bag, from his father, a medicine man, which brought with it the responsibility of protecting the tribe.[10] Made of animal skins or fabric, such bags contained amulets, charms, medicines, and other articles that provided the appropriate bearer with supernatural and medicinal power.

Tensions in the region escalated following an 1825 treaty signed at Prairie du Chien that established boundaries of white settlement and the territories of various Indian tribes in the region. Instead of reducing tensions, intertribal warfare and attacks on settlers increased. Throughout 1826 and 1827, some Ho-Chunk warriors and others launched a series of attacks along the Mississippi River and surrounding lands. One man present at the murder of a Prairie du Chien family was holy man and visionary White Cloud (Wabokieshiek), also called the Winnebago Prophet (Figure 1.3). Of mixed Sauk and Ho-Chunk ancestry, White Cloud led a little-known cultural revitalization movement focusing on a return to traditional ways. He lived with followers on the Rock River at the present Prophetstown, Illinois. Some of the perpetrators of

FIGURE 1.3

Portrait of Wabokieshiek, or White Cloud the Winnebago Prophet, by Robert Sully, 1833

WHi Image ID 79800

the Prairie du Chien attacks were arrested and some later executed, but White Cloud received a pardon and went on to become Black Hawk's close adviser, remaining with him to the bitter end.

The violence of 1827, which became known as the Winnebago Uprising, greatly alarmed settlers and federal officials even though relatively few individuals were involved. As a result, the federal government beefed up the presence of federal troops and built Fort Winnebago at the strategically important portage between the Fox and Wisconsin Rivers (modern-day Portage, Wisconsin) to better guard the frontier. Settlers formed volunteer companies of the Iowa County regiment of the Michigan Territory militia, under the command of Colonel Henry Dodge. The Ho-Chunk were pressured to cede land to the United States in the lead-mining region to accommodate this enterprise; the settlement it brought had the effect of creating more resentment and tension between the settlers and the Native Americans.

Black Hawk and his band continued to return to Saukenuk after their winter hunts even in the face of white settlement of their village lands. In 1831 militia forcibly expelled his band from Illinois and, according to another agreement dictated by the US government that year, they were not to return. Black Hawk reluctantly agreed to this, but plans for a return to reclaim ancestral lands soon began to form. Some disaffected Kickapoo, Fox, and Ho-Chunk people joined with Black Hawk's band in present-day Iowa, forming, in essence, a new tribe. Napope, a young, fiery Sauk civil chief, visited the British in Canada and claimed that the British promised assistance with supplies if trouble developed with Americans.

Several times during 1831 and 1832, Black Hawk consulted with White Cloud, who advised him from visions or dreams.[11] Dreams and visions by holy people had been hugely important to Indian people, especially in times of great stress. This was also the case in events involving Tecumseh, an Indian leader who led a multitribal uprising against the Americans in 1811 by following the visions of his brother, the Shawnee Prophet. Another much later example of such influences from the spirit world was seen in the Ghost Dance movement initiated by the visions of Wovoka, which swept the Great Plains in the late nineteenth century promising a magical deliverance from suffering caused by the whites and a return to a happy traditional life.[12] Prior to Black Hawk's decision to cross the Mississippi in violation of the 1831 agreement with federal authorities, White Cloud said that many tribes as well as the British would come to Black Hawk's aid. [13] Since this prediction came from the lips of a prophet, Black Hawk must have considered it prophecy.

Black Hawk Returns

Greatly encouraged by the alleged promises of support and the words of White Cloud, Black Hawk and a band of at least 1,100 crossed the Mississippi from what is now Iowa to Illinois on April 2, 1832, to reclaim their ancestral lands and cornfields. His followers were men, women, and children and included a formidable army of about five hundred warriors. How Black Hawk expected to resettle has long been a puzzle to historians. In his autobiography he claims peaceful intentions, and this is supported by the fact that he brought a large number of women and children with him. But surely his long and unhappy experience with Americans would have led him to expect great resistance, if not violence. In 1831 he had sent messengers on a secret mission to tribes in the north and others to the south, as far away as Arkansas and Texas; this hints that a general uprising against the Americans, much like Tecumseh's war, was being considered. On the other hand, Black Hawk and others may have simply believed that a large show of force would be sufficient to convince the Americans to let the band resettle in peace. [14] Mysticism also played a large role; however it actually occurred—through peace or war—resettlement on ancestral lands had been virtually foretold by the Winnebago Prophet. In addition, Black Hawk carried with him a powerful magical weapon: the great medicine bag from his father, which was "the soul of the Sauk Nation." [15]

In response to Black Hawk's move eastward across the Mississippi River, Governor Reynolds of Illinois called up two thousand militia volunteers (Figure 1.4) and alerted the Michigan Territory militia headed by Colonel Dodge. General Henry Atkinson, head of federal troops at Fort Armstrong at Rock Island, initially delayed action in an attempt to understand Black Hawk's intent, but he soon led troops to intercept the band. The militia and army sought to return Black Hawk to the other side of the Mississippi.

Black Hawk did not try to reclaim his home village of Saukenuk, a short distance from federal Fort Armstrong; instead, at the invitation of White Cloud, he traveled up the Rock River to the Winnebago Prophet's village to plant corn and perhaps resettle. Atkinson sent Indian subagent Henry

FIGURE 1.4

Drawing of Illinois volunteer militia, with volunteer Abraham Lincoln pictured at far left

Drawing by H. Charles MacBarron in *Military Collector and Historian* 18, no. 3 (1966): 87

Gratiot to the village to convince Black Hawk to return to the west side of the Mississippi River, but Black Hawk was not persuaded. Gratiot was menaced by zealous young warriors anxious to fight all comers. Thanks to the intervention of Black Hawk, who seemed intent on a peaceful resettlement, he escaped with his life, though barely. Unknown to Gratiot, Ho-Chunk chiefs accompanying Black Hawk urged him to continue ascending the Rock River, where reinforcements—"sufficient to repulse any army"[16]—were ready to fight alongside Black Hawk.

FIGURE 1.5

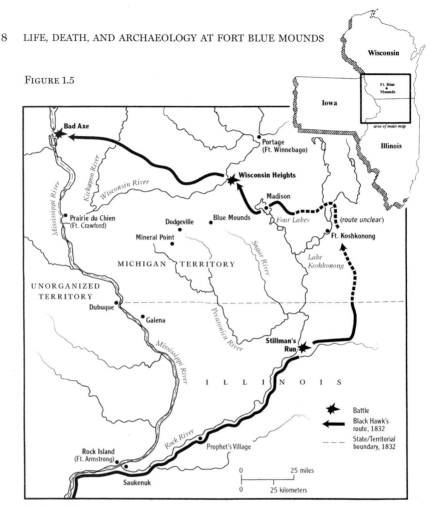

Fort Blue Mounds and the Black Hawk War, 1832

Map by Amelia Janes and Robert A. Birmingham

The Chase

With troops closing in, Black Hawk slowly moved his large band up the Rock River, awaiting the promised assistance (Figure 1.5). He eventually found that he had been misled by everyone. There was no word from the British, and the plight of his people stimulated no general uprising or major material support from area tribes. Some Ho-Chunk men later joined his band of warriors and others were in clear sympathy with Black Hawk's cause, but leaders of many Ho-Chunk villages turned out to be unenthusiastic, seeking to keep their people out of danger—sometimes by placating both sides. Indeed, while some Native American warriors used the atmosphere of war to attack settlers because of their own grievances against the Americans, several hundred men from midwestern tribes joined the Americans to fight against Black Hawk because of ongoing intertribal conflicts created by European and American settlement pressures or to curry favor with the Americans for political and material gain.[17]

Sensing the futility of the situation, Black Hawk attempted to have a parley with a volunteer company of the Illinois militia under the command of Major Isaiah Stillman with the intent of returning to the west side of the Mississippi in peace. A small party with a white flag was rebuffed by panicky militia volunteers, leading to a confrontation near modern-day Stillman Valley, Illinois, that routed the company, killing twelve militia men. Several of Black Hawk's warriors were also killed in the melee, today known as Stillman's Run because of the rapid retreat of the militia.

Now mired in conflict, Black Hawk led his band northeastward into what is now the state of Wisconsin. The band evaded militia and the US Army for several months, hiding in the marshy country of the Rock River headwaters in what is now south-central Wisconsin. Some Ho-Chunk—ostensibly American allies—misled the troops as to Black Hawk's whereabouts. In Washington, DC, President Andrew Jackson became so frustrated with the army's inability to stop, or even find, Black Hawk that he formally replaced Atkinson with General Winfield Scott and called up reinforcements. Neither Scott nor the reinforcements arrived before the conflict drew to a bloody end.

From his camps, Black Hawk sent out war parties in all directions to avenge Stillman's attack and secure provisions for the starving band. Black Hawk himself led a raid on a settlers' fort on the Apple River in northwest Illinois, two days from his location at the time.[18] This incident further illustrates the role that cultural mandates such as reprisals to restore honor—in addition to dreams and the belief in spirit powers—played in Black Hawk's often-puzzling decisions and movements.

In mid-July 1832, Black Hawk turned his band—with many members suffering from hunger and exhaustion—westward through the Four Lakes region and present-day Madison, Wisconsin, with the idea of descending to the Mississippi back to the safety of the Sauk settlement in modern-day Iowa.

Dodge's Michigan Territory militia, however, picked up Black Hawk's trail, which by this time was littered with discarded baggage and the corpses

Figure 1.6

Nineteenth-century painting of the Wisconsin Heights battlefield by Brookes and Stevenson. The Wisconsin River is the background.

of those who died of hunger or exhaustion. Along with the Illinois militia, Dodge raced ahead of the federal army. In the Madison area, the militia executed stragglers: one elderly man grieving at the grave of his wife was killed and scalped by a particularly cruel militia volunteer who was an Illinois newspaper editor in ordinary life.[19]

The militia caught up with the rear of Black Hawk's band on the afternoon of July 21 in the bluffs overlooking the Wisconsin River. The militia camped for the night, and in the predawn hours, the Sauk civil chief Napope called out to soldiers, pleading with them to allow the band to continue on so they could recross the Mississippi River and return to present-day Iowa in peace. Once more the conflict could have ended, but an interpreter was not available and the words fell on deaf ears. The next day, in the brief but intense confrontation known as the Battle of Wisconsin Heights (Figure 1.6), Black Hawk's outnumbered men fought a delaying action to allow women and children to flee across the river. Ironically, the battle took place within a short distance of what, in the mid-1700s, had been a major Sauk village on the Wisconsin River at present-day Sauk City, Wisconsin.[20]

Black Hawk lost many men, while the Americans suffered only one casualty. Despite this, the militia had failed to stop Black Hawk and bring the conflict to conclusion. Some of Black Hawk's band left the main group, heading down the Wisconsin where many died or were captured. Napope also left the band, taking refuge at a Ho-Chunk village, much to Black Hawk's puzzlement and anger. Napope had been the one who promised that the British would send supplies. Instead, the forsaken band was starving and reduced to melting lead ornaments to make musket balls.[21]

Massacre at Bad Axe

Black Hawk's success in eluding the Americans was short-lived. Atkinson and his federal troops caught up with the militia at Blue Mounds, where the militia had headed to regroup, and the combined forces chased the starving and decimated band northwest across rugged terrain toward the Mississippi River. Reaching the river on August 1 near its confluence with the Bad Axe River, Black Hawk found that the federal gunboat *Warrior* had been sent to block the band from crossing the river. Once again, Black Hawk attempted to parley, but much confusion ensued and the boat—armed with cannon and other weapons—opened fire, cutting down men, women, and children.

With troops closing in from the east, most of the band was determined to cross the river to escape the soldiers, but Black Hawk and some followers, including White Cloud, moved north to seek sanctuary among some Ojibwe. At one point Black Hawk changed his mind and sought to rejoin the main band, but then changed his mind again, resuming his movement north. The ostensibly self-serving abandonment of his people angered surviving members of the band at the time and remains a puzzle to modern historians. Certainly, the great warrior was not one to shy from a fight, and he had previously indicated his belief that he had the responsibility, as symbolized by his medicine bag, to protect his people. Perhaps visions, dreams, and prognostication led him to believe that ultimate success lie to the north. Perhaps he still followed the guidance of the Winnebago Prophet and holy man White Cloud, despite the fact that his advice had only led to disaster.

The next day, the gunboat returned. Caught on August 2 between the federal gunboat and the advancing troops, most of the remaining band were either massacred or drowned while crossing the river (Figures 1.7, 1.8a and b). The Dakota Sioux, allies of the Americans, awaited those who made the crossing, killing or capturing members of the band who reached the opposite bank. Black Hawk and his company later surrendered to some Ho-Chunk and were taken as prisoners to Fort Crawford at Prairie du Chien. In a sadly symbolic gesture, Black Hawk gave his medicine bag—"the soul of the Sauk Nation"—to one of the chiefs of the Mississippi River Ho-Chunk village where he had been taken. Black Hawk requested that it be turned over to the "American chief." The Ho-Chunk leader responded that he would instead keep it and return it if Black Hawk survived.[22]

Aftermath

Similar to other nineteenth-century Native American resistance and revitalization movements that sought a magical restoration of a former life, Black Hawk's own vision came to a violent end. He was imprisoned for a time and then given a tour of the East Coast, where he was treated as a celebrity. He was viewed with terror on the frontier, but the Eastern public admired his valiant efforts on behalf of his people. Afterward, he lived quietly in what is now Iowa until his death in 1836.

FIGURE 1.7

1856 painting of the Bad Axe massacre site by Brookes and Stevenson

FIGURES 1.8A AND B

Top, painting of the Bad Axe massacre by Cal Peters. Bottom, illustration of the gunboat *Warrior* opening fire on Black Hawk's band crossing the Mississippi River.

Top, WHi Image ID 4522; bottom, undated painting by Arntz and Company in Lelia Wardwell, ed., *American Historical Images on File: The Native American Experience* (New York: Media Projects, 1991)

But anguish and suffering continued for Native Americans living on the rich agricultural lands in what is now southern Wisconsin. In the wake of the Black Hawk War, the federal government quickly pressured the Ho-Chunk and Potawatomi to relinquish remaining claims to these lands and to relocate to western "Indian lands." Some resisted relocation; the Ho-Chunk of Wisconsin and the Forest County Potawatomi are their descendants. The treaties and removals, however, opened the door to a flood of white settlement. In this light, the Black Hawk War can be viewed as the major factor leading to the formation of the state of Wisconsin in 1848.

~ *2* ~

LIFE & DEATH
AT FORT BLUE MOUNDS

BLACK HAWK'S MOVEMENTS and the subsequent reports of battles and attacks threw the frontier settlers of the lead-mining region of the western Michigan Territory and the farm lands of northern Illinois into a state of frenzy and panic. New militia companies were formed, and the settlers took refuge in hastily erected stockades and fortified strongholds. They also took cover in federal forts such as Fort Crawford at Prairie du Chien on the Mississippi River and Fort Dearborn at Chicago. Some fled the region altogether. At Galena, Illinois, on the Fever River, the population was "perfectly panic struck," with women and children "rushing in from all parts of the country to go off in steam boats."[1] A later historical account described the scene at the settlers' Fort Holcomb: "women with disheveled locks were praying, men palsied with fear, and children screaming with affright."[2]

Although such accounts may be touched with a bit of hyperbole, the scale of the panic is quite evident by the fact that at least seventy-eight temporary fortifications were quickly built by frightened settlers, with a few even constructed in Indiana and Michigan (see appendix II). Judging from historical records, most of the white population of northern Illinois and the western Michigan Territory left their homes, mines, and farms in the late spring of

1832 to seek cover, and thousands of men volunteered to serve in Illinois militia and Michigan territorial militia.

Settlers of Blue Mounds Make a Fort

The miners and other settlers in the western Michigan Territory lead-mining district built at least twenty fortifications. Companies of several hundred mounted militia or rangers under the command of Colonel Henry Dodge rode the old Indian trails to provide cover for settlements and forts. Mounted couriers or "expresses" transmitted information between forts and the military about the movements of Black Hawk's band and accompanying violence.

Beginning about May 10, 1832, miners and settlers quickly constructed a log military fort at Ebenezer Brigham's lead mines on a prairie knoll just

FIGURE 2.1

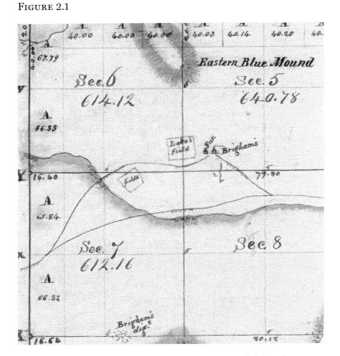

Part of 1833 land survey plat map showing trails, Brigham's establishment, and Brigham's diggings. The fort was built on a hill at the diggings marked at the bottom of the map.

Wisconsin Public Land Survey Records, Wisconsin Board of Commissioners of Public Lands

south of tall twin geological formations bearing the name Blue Mounds (Figures 2.1 and 2.2). The fort was located one and one-half miles from the tiny lead-mining community founded by Brigham on the south slope of the eastern prominence of the Blue Mounds. This was the first white settler community established in what is now Dane County, Wisconsin.

In 1822 Brigham, a native of Shrewsbury, Massachusetts, came to the lead-mining district, where he worked first as a prospector and later, in 1827, as a miner at Platteville (Figure 2.3).[3] During the Winnebago Uprising he built some sort of fortification at Platteville referred to only as a "blockhouse" for protection. He came to Blue Mounds in 1828, joining some miners and traders already working at the eastern edge of the mining district. He had attended a council at Green Bay that set boundaries between Indian lands and those that could be used for settlement and mining.

Brigham's buildings occupied land between a large spring and a major Indian trail, used by settlers as a road, which transected the lead-mining district and led to the federal Fort Winnebago, the major supply station for settlers. (The old trail would later become part of the Military Road, Wisconsin's

FIGURE 2.2

Photo of the Fort Blue Mounds site, 1991, with the western prominence of Blue Mounds in the background

FIGURE 2.3

Paintings of Ebenezer Brigham as a young man (inset) and in his later years

WHS Museum 1942.38; inset, WHi Image ID 2553

first highway.) From here, Brigham operated a roadside inn and store, lead-mining business, and fur trade with local Ho-Chunk people. He officially served as commissary to the Fort Blue Mounds militia company.

Construction of the fort was completed in less than two weeks and around May 20 all of the miners and other settlers in Blue Mounds moved in—no fewer than fifty people in all, including some children and an infant. Most were lead miners who worked for Brigham or his partners, Henry Starr and Esau Johnson; Johnson had a farm and a smelter next to Brigham's place.

There were not many other settlers in the area at the time. Among them were John Messersmith and his family, who came from a new farm sixteen miles west of Blue Mounds and stayed at the fort for three weeks, later relocating to Henry Dodge's fortification at Dodgeville, and lead miner Thomas McCraney and his family, who moved to the fort from their place west of Blue Mounds after June 20.[4] Militia volunteers and officials from elsewhere were assigned to the fort. Indian subagent Henry Gratiot, from Gratiot's Grove near the Illinois border, and Quebec-born Edward Beouchard, a miner and fur trader from Mineral Point, spent much time at the fort. Many others came and went, including members of other militia companies.

Beouchard, Messersmith, and Johnson left accounts that include descriptions of the fort and the major events it witnessed. Ebenezer Brigham wrote a "Memorandum of Passing Events," dated June 23, 1832, that provides a very brief summary of events in weeks prior, although some dates are incorrect. (The original, Figure 2.4, is now in the collections of the Wisconsin Historical Society as part of the Ebezener Brigham Papers.)[5] The other accounts were written well after the Black Hawk War and, as so often happens with recollections, sometimes the information is not completely accurate. However, official correspondence, dispatches, and records regarding the Black War and Fort Blue Mounds preserved in Whitney's *The Black Hawk War, 1831–1832* help clarify matters in some cases.[6] The archaeological work conducted at the sites provides an objective test of some types of information, such as the size and arrangement of the forts.

Eyewitness accounts describe a large log stockade constructed in a familiar frontier military pattern. Beouchard said that the 16- to 17-foot-high walls were 150 feet long with two corner blockhouses, each 20 feet square. This enclosed a storehouse and barracks that was 20 by 30 feet. In his memoirs, Johnson provided somewhat similar measurements, but he said that the 26-foot-by-30-foot blockhouses were two stories, and added that he and his wife, Sally, and their newborn infant moved into one blockhouse, while the unmarried Ebenezer Brigham took the other with his hired hand William Aubrey, Aubrey's wife, and their three children.[7]

Johnson dictated his recollections of the Black Hawk War in his elderly years, many decades after the fact, and these contain much detail concerning events at the fort during the war. However, the memoirs are full of embellishments, especially with regard to Johnson's role and activities at the fort.

FIGURE 2.4

Page from Brigham's diary entitled "Memorandum of Passing Events"

Ebenezer Brigham Papers, Wisconsin Historical Society

According to Johnson it was his idea to form a company and build the fort, and he supplied the timber. Moreover, he was the strongest man at the fort and the most steady, and he once stood off twenty men of the company who wanted his horse. Johnson was obviously a genuine frontier character, among many, and his memoirs add much color to the story of Fort Blue Mounds, even if they have to be read cautiously for historical detail.

A Company Is Formed

Forty-two men from the Blue Mounds area formed the Iowa County company of the volunteer Michigan Territory militia on May 20, according to the muster roll in the collection of the Wisconsin Historical Society (Figure 2.5). Colonel Henry Dodge came to drill the men, emphasizing the strategic importance of the fort: it was the closest fortification of any kind to Black Hawk's trail, and therefore it would be needed as a depot for provisioning pursuing troops. For this reason, Dodge instructed the settlers not to flee.[8]

FIGURE 2.5

MUSTER ROLL of Captain John Shermans Company of Iowa Militia Stationed at Blue Mounds Fort under Command of Col. _____ called into the service of the United States on the requisition of Gen. Henry Atkinson 20th May 1832.

1.	John Sherman	Captain	May 20th	3 Months
2.	George Force[1]	1st Lieut.	"	1 Month
3.	R. E. Collins	2d "	"	3 Months
4.	W. H. Haughton	1st Sergt.	"	"
5.	Henry Starr	2d "	"	"
6.	Moses Collins	3d Sergt.	"	"
7.	A. G. Haughton	4th "	"	"
8.	Esau Johnson	1st Corpl.	"	"
9.	R. S. Lewis	2d "	"	"
10.	Daniel Evans	3d "	"	"
11.	Jacob Keith	4th "	"	"
12.	Ebenezer Brigham	A. A. Commissary	"	"
13.	W. G. Auberry[2]	Private	"	17 Days
14.	Harvey Brock	"	"	3 Months
15.	Hugh Bowen	"	"	"
16.	Robert Creighton	"	"	"
17.	Samuel Davis	"	"	"
18.	John Dannels[3]	"	"	"
19.	John Dalby	"	"	"
20.	Moses Forman	"	"	"
20.	Anson Frazier	"	"	"
21.	Jonathan Ferril	"	"	"
22.	James Fiddick[4]	"	July 20	1 Month
23.	Emerson Green[5]	"	May 20	1 Month
24.	James Hanlon	"	"	3 Months
25.	Charles Harris[6]	"	"	1 Month

1   In remarks on muster roll, "Killed by the Enemy 20th June three miles from the Fort."
2   In remarks on muster roll, "Killed by the Enemy June 6th one mile from the fort."
3   Listed as Daniels on Pay Roll.
4   In remarks on Pay Roll, "Paid in Moores."
5   In remarks on muster roll, "Killed by the Enemy 20th June four miles from the Fort."
6   In remarks on Pay Roll, "Paid in Moores."

26.	J. C. Kellogg	Private	May 20	3 Months
27.	French Lake	"	"	"
28.	Jeremiah Lycan	"	"	"
29.	Thomas McCraney	"	"	"
30.	Fernando McCraney	"	"	"
31.	Jason Putnam	"	"	"
32.	James Prideaux[7]	"	July 20	1 Month
33.	William Prideaux[8]	"	"	"
34.	Jefferson Smith	"	May 20	3 Months
35.	Alpha Stevens	"	"	"
36.	William Stoney	"	July 20	1 Month
37.	Thomas Wilson	"	May 20	3 Months
38.	Samuel Woodworth	"	"	"
40.	Jno Messersmith[9]	"	"	1 Month
41.	Geo Messersmith[10]	"	"	"
42.	Wm Messersmith[11]	"	"	"

Entire company from Iowa County.[12]

I CERTIFY, on honor, that this muster roll exhibits the true state of Capt. John Sherman's Company of Iowa Militia in the service of the United States, for the period herein mentioned; that the "Remarks" set opposite the names of each officer and soldier, are accurate and just; and that the Recapitulation exhibits, in every particular, the true state of the Company.

John Sherman Capt

Commanding the Company

I CERTIFY, on honor, that I have carefully examined this muster roll, and that I have this 20th day of Aug 1832, mustered out of the service of the United States, the above mentioned Company of Iowa Militia by order of General Atkinson

W. W. Woodbridge

Adj & Insp Iowa Militia

7   Listed as Priddix on Pay Roll.

8   In remarks on Pay Roll, "Paid in Moores."

9   In remarks on Pay Roll, "Paid on Captain Gehons roll from."

10   In remarks on Pay Roll, "Paid on Captain Gehons roll from."

11   In remarks on Pay Roll, "Paid on Captain Gehons roll from."

12   The muster roll content has been produced verbatim. The number 20 appears twice in the original and number 39 is missing.

John Sherman is listed as captain of the company on the muster roll, but there is some confusion in the historical accounts as to when he took command. Beouchard and Messersmith recounted that Aubrey had been given initial command and that Sherman had been elected captain after Aubrey was killed on June 6. Beouchard further states that he, as first lieutenant, assumed command after Aubrey's death until Sherman was elected captain. However, dispatches sent before Aubrey was killed are signed by Sherman as captain.[9] It seems likely that Aubrey, who is listed as a private on the May 20 muster role, had been given charge of building the fort, but that Sherman had been elected to head the company when it was officially formed. Aubrey may have had some skills or prior military experience that led to this assignment. A William Aubrey is listed among militia volunteers out of federal Fort Armstrong at Rock Island, Illinois, the year before, in 1831.

Having built their defensive structure, the company turned its concerns to weapons since the men had only a few rifles, shotguns, and pistols among them. Despite an increasing number of conflicts with Native Americans and the presence of militia units and federal troops, the settlers of Illinois and present-day southwestern Wisconsin had few weapons themselves and sometimes had to make wooden clubs for defense. In some cases outside of the lead region, pewter household items were melted down to make balls for the few available guns.[10] Johnson's embellished memoirs contain an amusing, if unlikely, story about efforts to construct a cannon of lead at Fort Blue Mounds: the prototype blew to pieces when fired. According to Johnson, another cannon was fashioned, this time reinforced with metal straps. Loaded with nails and other debris, it blasted a wooden door set up quite some distance away. It is hard to know if this actually happened since it is not mentioned by others from the fort who left their accounts. However, there is another account, also unverified, that small cannons (2 pounders) were cast from lead at Fort Hamilton.[11]

In early June the men learned that cannons and swivels guns were available at an arsenal at Galena, Illinois,[12] and eventually several members of the group traveled there in wagons—a distance of nearly seventy miles. According to Johnson, who says he was among the men, they came away with a blunderbuss (a short shotgun with a flared muzzle) and a "6 pounder" (a reference to a small military field cannon that threw a 6-pound ball, or the equivalent, in shot)—but only after Johnson had threatened the men of the fort with an order to obtain the cannon, which was not generally distributed to militia.[13] On the way back they stopped at Mineral Point's Fort Jackson where, again according to Johnson, he thwarted an attempt by men there to steal the blunderbuss.

Military records of the US quartermaster stationed at Fort Jackson show that a single swivel gun was signed out to the "Mound Fort" on June 11.[14] Swivel guns were usually oversized, large-caliber flintlock guns mounted on swivels largely for use on boats, but the term also referred to similarly mounted blunderbusses and small cannons also in use at the time. Either Johnson's blunderbuss or cannon could be that swivel gun in the records. It most likely would have been mounted somewhere on the fort wall.

The same quartermaster records indicate that US muskets and accoutrements had been distributed to mounted militia or rangers assigned to Fort Blue Mounds for a time to augment the Blue Mounds force, but none appear to have fallen into the hands of the local fort defenders. Repeated requests to Dodge for arms and provisions went unheeded, prompting Brigham to write in his June 23 "Memorandum of Passing Events" that Dodge "appears to bear malice against [us?; page torn] for no cause."[15] In all likelihood, Dodge and other military authorities were bombarded with such requests from other forts and companies, since the miners and other settlers of the mining district had few arms.

According to Johnson, he and Brigham finally went to federal Fort Winnebago at the present-day Portage, Wisconsin, more than sixty miles away, where they secured a "wagon load" of used muskets needing repair. This quantity sounds suspiciously like another exaggeration,[16] and a check of surviving records of the Fort Winnebago quartermaster, although undoubtedly incomplete, failed to find a reference to the matter.

The Ho-Chunk and the Hall Girls

The Black Hawk War quickly engulfed the people of Fort Blue Mounds. Its position as the fort closest to Black Hawk's movements from late May through July made it the focus of frantic activity and violent death. Uncertain of the intentions of local Ho-Chunk bands and fearing they might side with Black Hawk, American officials called two councils with the principal chiefs of the region: the first, on May 26, at Lake Mendota near modern-day Madison and the second, two days later, at Blue Mounds.[17] The Ho-Chunk who lived in semiautonomous villages in northern Illinois and what is now southern Wisconsin played various roles in the Black Hawk War depending on kinship, personal relationships, political and economic ties, past grievances, and other factors.[18] Some joined Black Hawk or acted in clear sympathy with his cause; of these some occasionally feigned to side with the Americans. Others fought with the Americans, or served as scouts, as did some members of other tribes, including Potawatomi, Menominee, and Dakota Sioux. Many chose to stay out of the conflict completely. The Ho-Chunk leaders attending the councils assured the Americans of their peaceful intentions.

May 29 brought frightening news. A mounted carrier relayed the report of a fearsome attack on a settlers' homestead at Indian Creek near the Fox River in northeastern Illinois. Fifteen people were murdered, and two teenage girls, Rachel and Silvia Hall, were taken captive by Potawatomi warriors who used the atmosphere of war to settle personal grievances (Figure 2.6). The warriors turned over the girls to some Sauk men who had accompanied the Potawatomi warriors during the attack. General Henry Atkinson commanded Indian sub-agent Henry Gratiot to use his influence with the Ho-Chunk to obtain the girls' release from the Sauk, offering a large reward of horses and money.[19]

Edward Beouchard, who was acting as Indian subagent while Gratiot was away on other business, rode to the Ho-Chunk camp on the eastern

FIGURE 2.6

Capture of the Hall girls

WHi Image ID 11302

prominence of Blue Mounds, northeast of the Brigham residence, and talked to the Ho-Chunk leader Wa-kon-haw-kaw (Snake or Snakeskin), who in turn went to the chiefs of the Four Lakes region. After only a few days, the Ho-Chunk told Captain Sherman that the release of the girls had been secured and they would be handed over to the Americans. But the Ho-Chunk also passed on more terrifying news that confirmed the settlers' worst fears: two Sauk war parties had been dispatched to attack Fort Blue Mounds.[20]

On June 11, Beouchard rode out from the fort to meet the hostage release party along the main trail, on a high ridge at the headwaters of Sugar Creek, now known as Military Ridge, about eight miles east of the fort. (It is easy to ascertain the exact location of this meeting. Beouchard wrote that it took place where there were mounds in the shape of animals—ancient Indian effigy mounds. This would be the famous group, Figure 2.7, first mapped by R. C. Taylor in 1838, and the only such group of mounds in the area.[21] The major trail of the region passed through the mound group.) Dozens of Ho-Chunk escorted the girls, including several principal chiefs led by White Crow, orator and chief of the Ho-Chunk village on Lake Koshkonong. All then proceeded to Blue Mounds, where the girls, haggard but apparently healthy, were put in the care of women at the fort; Johnson later said his wife provided the girls with her own clothes.[22] Dodge came to the fort to take charge of the girls, who were later reunited with relatives in Saint Louis.

Death at Blue Mounds

The speed with which the Ho-Chunk obtained the release of the Halls no doubt made the Americans suspicious since it meant the Ho-Chunk maintained close contact with Black Hawk's elusive band. While staying at miners' cabins in Blue Mounds on the night of the release at Blue Mounds, some Ho-Chunk reportedly mocked the white settlers, saying that Black Hawk would defeat them. This prompted Dodge to take hostage those Ho-Chunk who had released the Hall girls in what can be characterized as an incredibly misguided attempt to guarantee peaceful behavior of local Indian people. Several Ho-Chunk leaders were taken to the farmstead and stopping place of James Morrison, near the present town of Ridgeway, west of Blue Mounds. There, another council was held, during which Dodge warned the Ho-Chunk to break all contacts with Black Hawk's band and keep peace with the Americans. They were later released at Gratiot's Grove.[23]

FIGURE 2.7

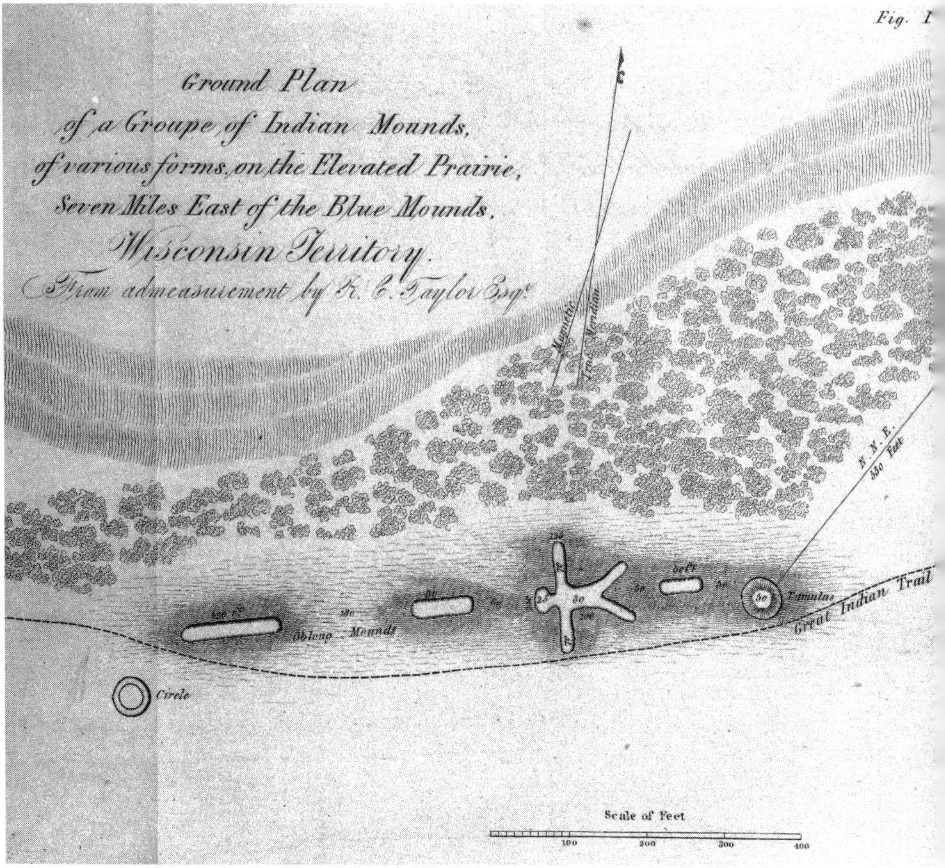

Ancient effigy mounds group along the trail where the Hall girls were released

WHi Image ID 5173

Indian subagent Gratiot attempted to appease the enraged men with horses and other gifts, but the insulting, disrespectful treatment that the Ho-Chunk endured exploded into violence within a week. On June 6, William Aubrey and Jefferson Smith, a member of the mining community and one of the Fort Blue Mounds militia volunteers, left the fort on horseback to get fresh water from the spring next to the Brigham establishment, a mile and a half from the fort (Figure 2.8). There, they were surprised by a small party of Indians who killed Aubrey on the spot, shooting him and spearing him in the neck. As told by Johnson, Smith ran back to the fort, blood flowing from

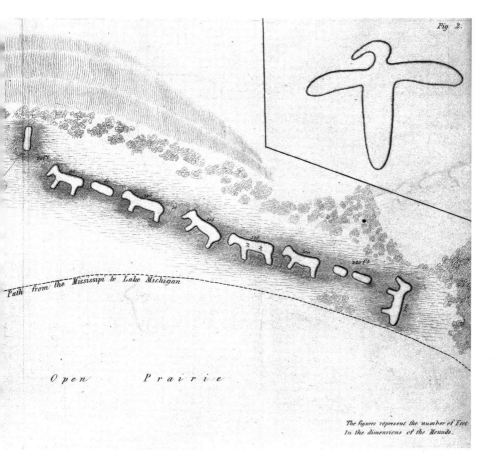

Fig. 2.

Path from the Mississippi to Lake Michigan

Open   Prairie

The figures represent the number of Feet
In the dimensions of the Mounds.

his nose. The attackers took the horses as well as a rifle and a pistol, both belonging to Ebenezer Brigham. Aubrey was buried on a high piece of prairie northeast of the fort "where it would be a nice place for a burying ground."[24]

The physical appearance of the attackers led the settlers to believe they were Ho-Chunk and not the Sauk warriors of Black Hawk's band, as has been expected. One militia man present at Fort Blue Mounds specifically attributed the attack to an earlier verbal altercation between Thick Lip, a Ho-Chunk man, and Aubrey's wife while she tended a garden, in which Thick Lip threatened to kill her husband.[25] Men of the fort and a mounted company of rangers

FIGURE 2.8

Spring area next to Brigham's establishment where Aubrey was killed

sent by Dodge followed a trail to Ho-Chunk leader Wa-kon-haw-kaw's abandoned camp on the side of the eastern prominence of the Blue Mounds (his
band had apparently left, seeking refuge from the conflict) and then to the
Wisconsin River, where the search was suspended. In a council convened after
the Black Hawk War, White Crow confirmed that some Ho-Chunk people had
indeed "raised the hatchet" against the Americans during the Black Hawk War
but named a different individual responsible for killing Aubrey.[26]

Anxiety increased at the fort through June as the defenders received
reports of bloody attacks and skirmishes in the lead-mining district as Black
Hawk's band moved north into Michigan Territory. The occupants awaited a
direct assault. Men had been killed at Kellogg's Grove in Illinois, and, on June
15, more were killed by a war party near Fort Hamilton at present-day Wiota,
Wisconsin, about thirty-five miles south of Blue Mounds. Hearing news of
the latter, Dodge rode to the Blue Mounds fort for fresh horses and then on
to Fort Hamilton, bringing with him militia and Ho-Chunk allies to repel
any remaining attackers. Beouchard also assembled a large group of sympa-
thetic Ho-Chunk men at Blue Mounds, who arrived at Fort Hamilton on foot

just after another man had been killed near the fort by a war party and after Dodge had already left in pursuit of the Indians. Dodge and his company of militia caught up with the war party on the Pecatonica River, killing all eleven members of the group in close combat.[27]

The Sauk war party the settlers had been expecting finally struck at the men of Blue Mounds on June 20 with deadly results. Patrolling the fort on horseback several miles east of the fort, Emerson Green and George Force were ambushed by a large party of Sauk warriors, possibly led by Ho-Chunk allied with Black Hawk's band.[28] Force was cut down immediately, but Green made for the fort. Within view of the fort's inhabitants, Green had his horse shot out from under him and was quickly surrounded. Beouchard went to retrieve the body and later wrote that Green had been scalped, beheaded, and dismembered, and his heart removed.[29] Mutilation of the dead and body-part trophy taking was practiced by both Indians and Americans in many frontier conflicts, including the Black Hawk War. Green's remains were carried in a blanket and buried "at the fort." Still lacking weapons at this point, Brigham noted in his diary on June 23 that "our situation is a delicate one, I expect an attack from the Indians [the word Indians is underlined twice], we cannot stand a siege."[30] Below that he provided information on where to contact his next of kin.

Force's body was left on the prairie for four days because the fort personnel—lacking guns—were too frightened to retrieve it. Dodge and a group of rangers discovered Force's remains, also horribly mutilated, and buried him alongside the main trail about two miles east of Blue Mounds.[31] Dodge left men at the fort for several days to stand guard and reconnoiter the area for further danger.

A Strategic Fort

Following the attacks, Fort Blue Mounds primarily operated as a supply center for the military pursuing Black Hawk, as Dodge predicted it would. Thirty-five wagonloads of supplies—gathered from depots at Mineral Point and Dixon's Ferry in Illinois—were assembled at the fort to be sent east in relief of Atkinson's troops.[32]

Ultimately headed toward the Mississippi, Black Hawk and his people made their way west to the Wisconsin River. There, on July 21, the Battle of Wisconsin Heights was waged along the river about fifteen miles north of Fort Blue Mounds. The conflict was close enough for Johnson to write that he rode out the next day to inspect the battle site and the dead bodies of Black Hawk's warriors.[33] Exhausted and low on provisions, the Illinois and Michigan Territory militias involved in that battle regrouped at Blue Mounds to rest, reprovision, and treat several wounded. The militias stayed for several days and later were joined by General Atkinson and his US Army regulars. At one point, more than one thousand soldiers camped in the vicinity of the fort as they readied themselves to continue the chase and bring the conflict to a climax. Among them was Meriwether Lewis Clark, aide-de-camp to General Atkinson and son of William Clark of Lewis and Clark expedition fame. From Blue Mounds, he sent a letter containing maps of Black Hawk War campaign areas to his famous father, who had become the superintendent of Indian affairs in the War Department.[34]

The War Passes By

Black Hawk's trail was quickly identified, and the combined military forces of militia and army left in pursuit. When the soldiers left, a welcome calm descended on the people of the fort as the war passed by. Following the reprehensible Bad Axe massacre and Black Hawk's subsequent surrender, the three-month Black Hawk War ended in August 1832. At the command of General Atkinson, the Blue Mounds Company of the Iowa County Michigan Territory militia was mustered out of service of the United States on August 20, 1832, and the lead miners and settlers returned to their homes and lives, no doubt greatly shaken by the experience.

Esau Johnson wrote that he arrived home to find his buildings and lead furnace dissembled and burned. He and his family returned to the fort to live while his home was rebuilt.[35] He later moved to Dodgeville, Wisconsin. Lead mining continued for several decades more at Brigham's diggings. In his account book for November 22, 1832, Brigham lists supplies for the "Fort Establishment" and says four men had gone to live at the fort.[36] Mining continued in the area until about 1850, when the demand for lead, used mainly to make white paint for houses back East, had subsided. Brigham went on to serve in a number of local, territorial, and state offices. He left no direct descendants, but some of his original property remains in the hands of his brother's descendants. It is the site of the underground cavern that is now Cave of the Mounds, a popular attraction.

FIGURE 2.9

The fort's historical marker in 1991

Many miners of the region headed west during the California gold rush, starting in 1848. Edward Beouchard went back to live out his years in Mineral Point, publishing a defense of his character in the 1876 *Report and Collections of the State Historical Society of Wisconsin* in response to unflattering comments made about him in an article by Albert Salisbury entitled "Green County Pioneers," which had been published in the 1872 *Report and Collections of the State Historical Society of Wisconsin.*[36] Henry Gratiot went home to Gratiot's Grove. Still attentive to the Ho-Chunk, he died in 1836 returning from a personal mission to Washington, DC, to secure treaty annuity payments owed the tribe by the United States. One of Brigham's employees, William Houghton, returned to his native Indiana, where he died in 1886 after lifelong "mental anxiety and physical suffering" attributed to his three-month service in the Black Hawk War at Fort Blue Mounds.[37] His obituary refers to an unspecified injury. Vaulted to fame by his exploits in the Black Hawk War, Henry Dodge went on to become the governor of the Wisconsin Territory. The graves of Aubrey, Green, and Force have not yet been located.

Eventually, the stockade of Fort Blue Mounds was dismantled, its valuable wood needed to fuel lead-mine furnaces and for the construction of buildings in this area of extensive prairie. Swales and depressions marking the once important frontier fort were still visible when the Wisconsin Historical Society erected the historical marker in 1921, but even those traces eventually disappeared, eliminated by time and farming. One by one, the plowing of surrounding fields knocked over the cement markers the Wisconsin Historical Society had used to outline the property. By 1991 only the small historical marker remained in the middle of a farm field (Figure 2.9). Somewhere in the vicinity were the remains of Fort Blue Mounds waiting to be rediscovered.

3

Digging Fort Blue Mounds

On September 5, 1921, Wisconsin
Historical Society officials, local dignitaries, and residents of the modern village of Blue Mounds gathered to dedicate a brass plaque marking the site of Fort Blue Mounds. A quarter acre of the fort site—an island in the middle of farmland—had been donated to the Wisconsin Historical Society in 1910 by Brigham and Carrie Bliss of Blue Mounds. The historical marker was the first for the state agency (previously it worked through other organizations to mark historical and archaeological places), and reflected the efforts of an energetic landmarks committee and a new era of public outreach pioneered by Director Reuben Thwaites.[1]

Seventy years after the dedication, Wisconsin Historical Society researchers visited the site to gather historical and archaeological evidence regarding the exact location and size of Fort Blue Mounds and to learn more about its construction and history. The nearly decade-long study enlisted scores of volunteers to assist in site survey, excavation, and mapping. This research resulted in the first detailed description of the fort and its place in Wisconsin history.

The Environment of the Fort Blue Mounds Site
The first goal of our archaeological project was to determine the exact location of the quarter-acre property that had been donated to the Wisconsin

Historical Society. On that land would be some part of a large fort that historical records stated was 150 feet on each side. It was obvious from the historical marker that the general location of the fort was in the surrounding area, but exactly where the fort was in relationship to the marker was unknown.

In 1832 the miners of the Blue Mounds community had selected a high hill at Ebenezer Brigham's lead diggings on which to build the fort. This was the highest point in the prairie south of the Blue Mounds, "commanding an extensive view of the open country for many miles" in the words of Edward Beouchard.[2] The location next to the mines also offered a large supply of lead that could be melted into ammunition (Figure 3.1). One problem, though, was water. The only water supply is a small drainage west of the hill that likely would have dried up in the summer months. Instead, water was obtained, at least initially, from a spring a mile and a half from Brigham's establishment and would have been kept in barrels at the fort. After the June 6, 1832, attack on men getting water at the spring, it is likely that further attempts to get water were made under heavy guard. No well was mentioned, or has yet to be discovered, at the fort site; it would have had to been cut deep through bedrock. It is also possible that groundwater in the adjacent deep mine shafts could have been used. The long-term effects of lead poisoning were not known at the time, and, in any case, it would have seemed the least of the problems facing the settlers.

The core of the hill is dolomite and sandstone bedrock formed under ancient seas more than 440 million years ago. Into this bedrock, mines were sunk in search of lead, which occurs as small cubes commonly called galena. Ironically, the lead mines in the area may have first been worked by Black Hawk's ancestors when they lived in Wisconsin. The French explorer Jonathan Carver reported that in 1766 the Sauk living on the Wisconsin River north of Blue Mounds at present-day Sauk City obtained lead somewhere in this area.[3] Native Americans used lead to make the white paint they applied as body decoration. During the early nineteenth century a large market developed in the East for white paint for clapboard houses, leading to a rush to the lead region of the Midwest. Europeans and Americans as well as Indians used lead to make ammunition for guns during this period.

At the Fort Blue Mounds site, the bedrock is mantled by a soil classified as a silty loam.[4] Nodules of chert—a hard, flintlike stone—are found throughout the soil, leftovers from higher layers of rock that eroded away in the ancient

FIGURE 3.1

Trees grow around one of Brigham's old mines along the east of the Fort Blue Mounds site.

past. Geological history also accounts for different subsoils within a short distance. The bedrock of the region is mainly dolomite, a carbonate-rich rock formed under the tropical sea, which is underlain at some depth by sandstone. The contact between rock units, however, is uneven. In the far eastern part of the Fort Blue Mounds site, our archaeological investigations found dolomite bedrock beneath the shallow (eight to fourteen inches) modern soil in the form of a dense layer of disintegrating dolomite bedrock. As we dug west of this, the soils deepened and the dolomite had completely weathered away to older sandstone. In this area we encountered a thick layer of fine sand approximately two-and-a-half feet from the ground's surface and extending down three to four feet to a layer of disintegrating sandstone bedrock from which the sand originated.

The variation in the depths of the bedrock was an important consideration during the planning and construction of the fort in that stockade posts had to be set firmly in the ground and deep defensive ditches had be dug. The builders placed one blockhouse where bedrock is closest to the surface on the site. The blockhouses were of horizontal log construction—like log cabins—and therefore little digging needed to be done. Where the soil was much deeper, the men of Fort Blue Mounds dug the stockade trench and defensive ditches.

The Archaeological Investigations

Because of the costs involved, especially for labor, an archaeological undertaking such as the one we planned would normally have to await major funding. However, in 1991 there was enormous public interest in archaeology, and our search for Fort Blue Mounds attracted many volunteers. Recruits initially came from the Charles E. Brown Archaeological Society, a group of people interested in archaeology who meet monthly at the Wisconsin Historical Society headquarters. After some newspaper publicity, many others came forward to donate their time and skills and to learn more about the early history of the state.

Many of the volunteers had long dreamed of participating in an archaeological "dig," but there were few such opportunities that didn't entail large investments of personal time and money. Most such public projects required long commitments and travel to far-off places, as well as costs for training and accommodations. In this case, volunteers could devote as much as they wanted to—even a few hours at a time—at a site almost literally in their backyards. The only cost for some was an occasional lunch at a nearby rural tavern, where finds of the day were discussed. Terry Genske, a land surveyor by profession and our volunteer surveyor, noted that the broken cement pillars that once marked the land had iron reinforcing rods, and reasoned that the bases of the broken pillars could be found in the ground using a metal detector (Figure 3.2). Terry, who often searched for property markers as a part of his job, located the bases of the four markers with amazing speed, thereby reestablishing the quarter acre of Wisconsin Historical Society land. He also found the broken base of a fifth marker set in from the outer square in the northwest part of the property. That marker would remain a mystery to us for a long time.

The next task, one that would be much more involved, was to locate the buried remains of the fort on the small Wisconsin Historical Society parcel of land. If historical accounts describing the size of the fort were correct, the original site would extend onto adjacent farm fields. With the cooperation of the neighboring landowners, the surfaces of surrounding plowed farmland were systemically searched for artifacts. The survey eventually included the

FIGURE 3.2

Upper left, land surveyor Terry Genske looks for old property markers. The other pictures show volunteers at work during the archaeological project.

use of a metal detector to locate metal objects, which would be abundant at a site such as this. Significantly, the land around the quarter-acre property yielded few artifacts that could be related to the fort—the first clue that the fort was smaller than early accounts suggested. The metal detector mainly found more recent farm-related objects, such as machinery, plow parts, and harness buckles.

Examination of the area was also undertaken with ground penetrating radar (GPR), a more sophisticated remote-sensing technology, which the

Wisconsin Geological and Natural History Survey provided for a day along with an operator, Walter Hall. GPR uses radar pulses to detect large objects, changes in soil density, and rock beneath the ground. Differences in radar reflection are called anomalies. The technology cannot, however, identify the nature of the anomalies. The results were intriguing but complicated by the geology and natural soil characteristics of the hill. Probing with a soil corer showed that, in some places, bedrock rose close to the surface and, in others, soil had accumulated in depressions and fissures. Both registered as anomalies that could be confused with underground disturbances related to the fort. One area of particularly strong and intriguing anomalies was selected for the first dig.

Major excavations always start with establishing a grid so researchers can later attribute unearthed artifacts to a particular spot and make maps of features. The grid used at Blue Mounds consisted of five-foot-by-five-foot units or squares that would be carefully excavated using shovels, trowels, and other archaeological tools (Figure 3.3). With the thought that the historical marker was placed near the center of the fort, we put a stake at the corner of the marker. This became the center of the grid and we designated it 0 North/South, 0 East/West. Terry tied this point to a section corner of the state property survey system so the location of the excavations would be permanently recorded.

The Fort Blue Mounds excavations began with two excavation units placed fifteen feet north and fifteen feet south of the historical marker. We selected the southern unit (N0 S15) on the basis of strong indications from the GPR of subsurface disturbances. Initial digging showed that the top eight inches of the site had been plowed, which had mixed and displaced artifacts and obliterated the tops of buried features such as the fort's stockade trench. In other similar situations, archaeologists simply bring in heavy, earth-moving bulldozers to scrape the disturbed zone off the entire site and quickly expose buried features. This method was used at two Black Hawk War fortifications in Illinois: the Apple River Fort at Elizabeth and Beggs's Fort at Plainfield.[5] However, we felt that all artifacts would provide critical information even if they were not in their original locations; experience has shown that while plowing displaces artifacts, the artifacts may not be very far from where they were initially deposited and so offer insights as to the places of various activities. Heavy, earth-moving equipment was not used until later

FIGURE 3.3

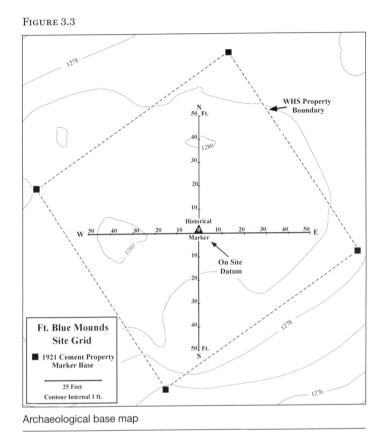

Archaeological base map

in our project—and then it was used judiciously. Volunteers shoveled through the disturbed plow zone at the Fort Blue Mounds site and then troweled the soil in four-inch levels to expose features and recover artifacts. All excavated dirt, including from the plow zone, was shaken through a quarter-inch mesh screen to recover small items that were missed during excavation.

The Fort Located

As any archaeologist can attest, luck often plays a role in an archaeological investigation. Even some great discoveries have been made by good fortune or happenstance. Beneath the plow zone in E0 S15, the team uncovered straight, dark soil discoloration one foot wide and several feet deep—a filled-in wall trench that once supported the vertical logs that formed the stockade or outer wall of the fort (Figure 3.4). The stockade trench, designated Feature 2, was discovered in an area where subsurface radar had indicated strong anomalies. But even so, coming right down on the wall that ran through the middle of the excavation unit was good fortune indeed.

Needless to say, locating a wall at the very start of the field project created much excitement, as did the discovery of numerous artifacts in that area: small pieces of dishware, musket balls and shot, lead, nails, white clay tobacco pipe pieces, and animal bone, as well as a dense scattering of tiny brick fragments and clay chinking of the type used to fill the spaces between log buildings (Figure 3.5). Lead in various forms would be a common find throughout the project since the occupants made their own ammunition—musket balls and shot—out of lead extracted from the adjacent mines.

With the stockade wall identified, it seemed a simple matter of following the wall around the fort perimeter using selected excavation units and other testing; this goal occupied the first two seasons of work. In one area of the trench (Figure 3.4), the rounded end of an individual oak log was still in place, and farther along the line to the southwest, circular stains, called post molds, marked the former location of posts.

FIGURE 3.4

The stockade trench, with a large rock and the remains of a wood post

FIGURE 3.5

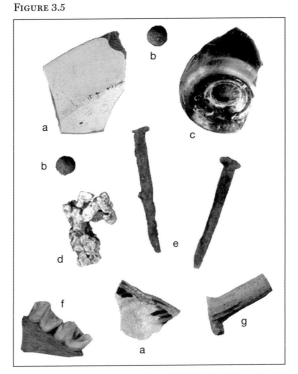

Typical artifacts: a) dishware sherds, b) shot, c) glass shard,
d) lead, e) nails, f) animal bone, and g) clay pipe fragment

Wisconsin Historical Society collections

Investigation along the wall trench line to the northeast showed that the trench sloped up sharply to the northeast and terminated a few feet from where it was discovered, at a point where bedrock rose close to the surface and the fort builders would have been unable to continue digging (Figure 3.6). Six feet from the end of the very shallow part of the trench's end, a large rock in the trench appeared to mark the end of where the wood posts of the stockade were placed in deeper soil—no doubt to wedge and anchor it in the soil. Approximately five feet out from the fort's log wall, another wider, deep, dark stain was found running parallel to the wall; it was later determined to be the shallow end of a filled-in defensive ditch that partly encircled the fort. It also terminated where bedrock rose near the surface of the ground.

We dug short, exploratory trenches northeast to see if the fort wall and defensive ditch resumed in deeper soil beyond the shallow soil overlaying bedrock, but they did not. Having found one corner of the fort, we reasoned that this was where the stockade and defensive ditch met one of the two corner blockhouses, described in historical documents, that were built of horizontal logs, much like old log cabins. The builders used this part of the site for a blockhouse since the wall trench and defensive ditch could not be easily cut into the bedrock there. The plowing of farm fields had destroyed

FIGURE 3.6

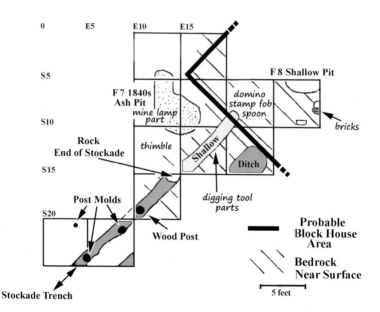

Map drawing showing the southeast stockade trench and defensive ditch and the east blockhouse area along with the locations of selected key artifacts. Left, the Fort Blue Mounds blockhouse would have been similar to this reconstructed one at the Apple River Fort in Elizabeth, Illinois.

any shallow impressions the bottom logs of the structure would have made in the soil.

A comparison of the location of the defensive ditch at the probable edge of the blockhouse and where the log stockade ended, marked by the large anchoring rock, suggested that there had been a several foot gap between the stockade and the blockhouse, as shown in Figure 3.6. This gap probably represents a narrow doorway alongside the building, which would have facilitated access to the lead mine immediately to the east.

Digging expanded into the area once occupied by the blockhouse. There, much domestic debris was unearthed: dishware fragments, eating utensils, buttons, a thimble, glass bottle fragments, and more animal bone. Scattered throughout the area were brick fragments and clay chinking broken into tiny pieces by modern plowing. Several bricks within the suspected blockhouse remained in place just below the plow zone; these were a probable base for a fireplace of some sort. Other artifacts were found below this area, an indication that the floor of the blockhouse extended deeper than the surrounding land surface.

A large, shallow pit, designated Feature 7, had been dug alongside the blockhouse and filled with ash, charcoal, and a small amount of refuse, both burned and unburned (Figure 3.7). Examination of dishware sherds found in this feature led to another early and significant discovery. A few pieces bore a decorative scene and pattern name, Texian Campaigne, which commemorated other wars: the 1835–1836 Texas war of independence from Mexico and especially the 1846–1848 conflict between the United States and Mexico over the possession of Texas and other lands in the southwest.[6] Obviously these had to have been deposited at the site long after 1832. This discovery provided the first archaeological evidence that the fort buildings had been subsequently used by miners for living quarters at the lead mines as Brigham's account book had suggested.

Two other artifacts discovered during the initial field seasons were especially exciting because they put the people who had lived at the fort in the mind's eye (Figure 3.8). One was a part of a digging tool, a shovel, or a pick part left in place in the stockade line, apparently broken by a frantic digger as he hit bedrock near the surface. This digger, like all the men working during the construction of the fort, knew that Black Hawk was heading their way and an attack could be expected at any time. The other is a most unusual object found below the plow zone in the area of the blockhouse: a broken but otherwise complete wax stamp with the letter *J* attached to a chain called a seal fob. Stamps like this with the initial of the sender were pressed on the melted wax used to seal letters. Seals on chains, or fobs, kept in a vest pocket were considered fashionable for men in the late eighteenth and early nineteenth centuries. It could well be a coincidence, but Esau Johnson said he and his family occupied a blockhouse during the war and returned to live at the fort for a time after.[7] Further details on this find and other Fort Blue Mounds artifacts are presented in the next chapter.

As the work neared the end of the third season, excitement became tempered with puzzlement and a little frustration as excavations proceeded at intervals along the stockade and defensive ditch to the southwest. Exploratory trenches showed that the stockade wall did not extend 150 feet, as suggested by the historical record, but turned to form the southwest wall a mere 40 feet from its start at the edge of the blockhouse. The fourth season started with the testing of a new idea: Fort Blue Mounds was much smaller than the historical accounts had led us to believe.

FIGURE 3.7

Excavation in progress on Feature 7, an ash-filled pit containing many artifacts. Bottom, sherd from an English-made Texian Campaigne series pattern plate found in the ash pit.

½ inch

FIGURE 3.8

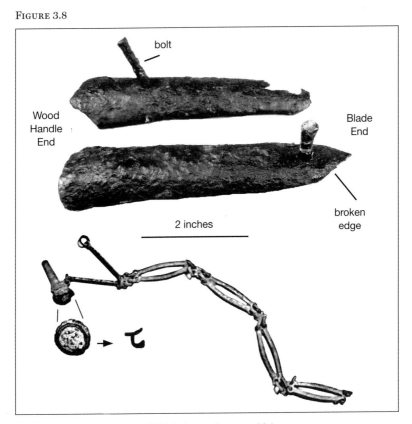

Broken digging tool parts and initialed wax stamp and fob

Wisconsin Historical Society collections

Defining the Fort

During the first three seasons of work, we had reestablished the boundaries of the state-owned Wisconsin Historical Society property and located parts of the fort itself: the southeast wall, the defensive ditch, and the eastern blockhouse area (Figure 3.9). We found hundreds of artifacts from the time of the Black Hawk War and from the years of occupation thereafter. The fourth season began in the summer of 1994 with the much-anticipated excavation of the south corner of the fort that had been located at the end of the previous season.

Here we found a neat right-angle turn in both the stockade line and the deeper defensive ditch, highlighted by light yellow soil below the darker plow

FIGURE 3.9

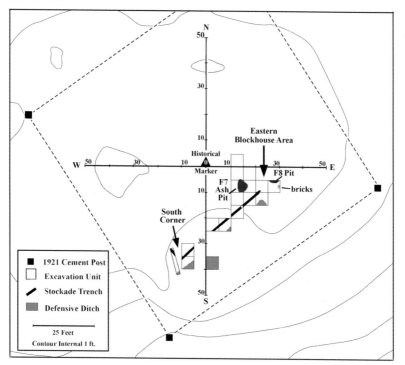

Archaeological map after the third season of work

zone (Figure 3.10). Few artifacts were discovered in the deep ditch, but among them was a broken, dark-green wine bottle and the jaw or mandible of a pig— onetime food and drink. The pig mandible lay at the very bottom of the ditch originally dug four feet to the top of the bedrock and could well have been thrown in over the wall during the fort's first occupation in 1832 (Figure 3.11). A large tusk, the modified canine tooth of the animal, was still in place in the jaw. Used by the pig for rooting up plant food and for defense, tusks are now cut by pig raisers to prevent injury to people and other pigs. Butchered pig bone found throughout the site indicates that pork was clearly an important food to the settlers who had lived there. The presence of many tusk pieces among the bone indicates that the pigs had been allowed to forage on their own.

We unearthed another piece of the Fort Blue Mounds puzzle at this south corner. A sixth base of a cement marker from 1921 remained deeply buried

FIGURE 3.10

South corner of the stockade line and the broken original cement fort marker

FIGURE 3.11

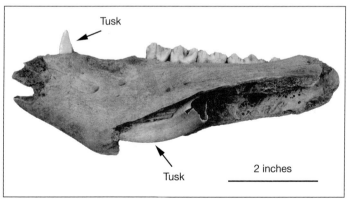

Mandible or jaw of a pig with a growing tusk found in the defensive ditch

along the filled-in defensive ditch (Figure 3.10). Previously, five others had been found, four of which defined the Wisconsin Historical Society property and a fifth one located inside of these in the north part of the property. This newly discovered one marked the south corner of the fort, leading us to the conclusion that an inner square of posts had once marked remains of the fort itself and had still been visible as depressions and ridges on the surface in 1921. The fifth marker found by Terry Genske early in our project would potentially then indicate the north corner of the fort. This would mean that the whole fort lay on Wisconsin Historical Society land.

Moving ahead again with short exploratory trenches, we located and carefully excavated the end of the southwest stockade trench of the fort forty-five feet from the second corner. As with the east corner of the fort, discovered earlier in the project, the stockade here simply stopped and the very end was packed with small rocks, obviously marking the area of a second blockhouse at the west corner of the fort (Figure 3.12). A major conclusion came from this evidence: the size of the fort had been much exaggerated in published recollections and, indeed, the entire fort was within the small

FIGURE 3.12

End of stockade trench at the west corner of fort

quarter-acre property donated to the Wisconsin Historical Society in the early twentieth century.

While the interior of the fort was not a main focus of the project, we sampled some areas during the fifth season of work to see if remains of the central building were preserved. A circular dark stain found five feet from the stockade wall proved to be the location of a large, long-decayed post, six inches in diameter, driven deep into the ground, which was probably a support post of the central structure of the fort. Small layers of ash in the vicinity suggested that the remains of the structure had been burned at some point.

With the general pattern of the fort and a large, if highly fragmentary, sample of artifacts recovered, in the sixth season we brought in a contractor to remove the plow zone in narrow trenches with a small bulldozer in selected

FIGURE 3.13

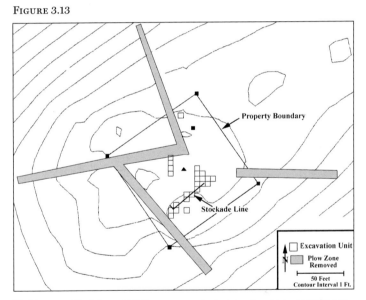

Right, a small bulldozer strips the plow zone in search of the north extent of the fort site. Top, map showing the location of the machine-stripping of the plow zone.

FIGURE 3.14

Stone rubble fill at the south end of the northwest defensive ditch, where it would have abutted the western blockhouse.

areas to quickly confirm our conclusion regarding the fort's size (Figure 3.13). The trenches exposed more features and artifact concentrations, but all within boundaries of the defined quarter acre.

Excavation units set up over the remains exposed by the plow-zone stripping contributed to our knowledge of the site. One ash layer turned out to be the top of a filled-in northwest defensive ditch, designated Feature 18, where it abutted the western blockhouse. Below it, at the bottom of the ditch, was a pile of dolomite rock, obviously mine rubble, intermixed with clay mortar and window glass. While the rock could simply be fill, it could also be the remains of a stone chimney added to the blockhouse years after the war. The rock pile was left in place for future investigation (Figure 3.14). At the south end of the defensive ditch, the base of yet another cement post was uncovered, marking the west corner of that feature.

Excavations of the ditch fill along the northwest edge of the fort yielded numerous artifacts found elsewhere at the site, including eating utensils, dishware, lead, shot, nails, buttons, clay pipe fragments, bottle glass, and animal bone, all likely gathered up with other debris from around the block-house when the ditch was filled. The fill also produced an unusual cluster of artifacts, among them glass beads like those used in the Indian fur trade, the back of a circular lead seal used to fasten bales of furs, and a silver coin (Figure 3.15). One explanation for the presence of trade objects is that Brigham him-self engaged in a trade with the Ho-Chunk and likely brought some items to the fort. The coin, a United States half dime bearing the date 1837, was a valu-able piece of evidence concerning the history of the fort in that it provided a date after which this part of the defensive ditch was filled.

As was the case with the blockhouse on the east corner, a gap in the stockade and defensive ditch lines represented the area of the blockhouse on the west. However, while some artifacts were found in the plow zone, the density was not nearly as high as that found in the eastern blockhouse area and few artifacts were found below this zone, which would have been part of the blockhouse floor. Among the items found in the floor area was a large-caliber musket ball. The fact that so few items were found suggests that this blockhouse floor had some kind of covering, probably wood planks. In contrast, judging by the large quantity of domestic debris deposited where the floor had been, the eastern blockhouse evidently had a dirt floor. One person who commanded the status and resources to have a wood floor was community leader Ebenezer Brigham, who, according to Esau Johnson, lived in one blockhouse along with the William Aubrey family.[8] Since the fill of the adjacent ditch likely included discarded and lost items from around the blockhouse, Brigham's presence here would explain the fur trade goods found in this part of the site.

Additional stripping by heavy machinery uncovered a layer of ash and a disintegrating brick platform in the interior of the fort, right next to the old historical marker. The remains, designated Feature 20, formed the base of a hearth or forge probably

FIGURE 3.15

½ inch

1837 silver coin from the fill of the northwest defensive ditch

Wisconsin Historical Society collections

associated with the central building. Slag, the byproduct of blacksmithing, was found in the vicinity, as well as an unusual quantity of lead in various forms, which indicates that the fort occupants used the area to melt lead before pouring it into gang molds to make lead balls.

A Fort-Site Dump

Machine-assisted stripping of the plow zone along the southwest stockade wall led us to discover the largest and most interesting part of the fort complex found during the project: designated Feature 16. Here, removal of the top one foot of soil exposed a part of the defensive ditch that widened to seven feet and had been filled with thick layers of ash, animal bone, and broken and discarded artifacts, some burned or melted, to the depth of bedrock at three feet below the surface (Figure 3.16). Like the adjacent stockade line, the feature terminated at what was the blockhouse, where it was neatly squared off.

Excavation of the top part of the feature unearthed a broken, blue-printed English-made plate. The English scene called "Villa in the Regent's Park, London" was printed on pearlware, a blue-hued fine earthenware made and

FIGURE 3.16

Excavated top of southwest defensive ditch, Feature 16, with sandstone pieces. Inset images, front and back of large sherd from Villa in the Regent's Park, London pattern transferprint plate found in the fill.

Inset, Wisconsin Historical Society collections

used into the early 1830s. Pearlware is a type of ceramic that would still have been in use during the Black Hawk War era. Although the ditch could have been used for the disposal of food remains and other garbage during the war, it is surmised that most of the filling took place just afterward, when people, returning to the site to live, cleared the debris, dismantled the walls, refurbished buildings, and burned the refuse. Two worn and burned fire-starting flints accompanied the ash and debris. Careful excavation of this remarkable feature could itself have occupied several seasons of work, but, after documenting the extent and recovering a sample of artifacts from the top two feet of the deposits, the feature was reburied, leaving a trove of information preserved for future exploration.

The Final Corner

During the brief final season of fieldwork, we followed the defensive ditch and stockade line along the southwest side of the fort toward the north and final corner. Based on the length of the fort on the opposing side and other information, we were able to predict the location of this corner and its appearance: it would look like the opposite south corner—a continuous wall with a right-angle turn. In addition, a cement marker had been placed near here in 1921, suggesting that this corner area, perhaps a depression of the defensive ditch, was somehow visible at the time.

On April 30, 2000, we climbed the hill with great excitement, anticipating finding the final corner of the stockade and bringing the field phase of the project to close. Digging and troweling furiously, we followed the last bit of stockade line to its end. There we found the final corner, making its right-angle turn, as predicted (Figure 3.17). Later in the summer, the last bit of excavation confirmed that the defensive ditch, originally dug to the top of bedrock at this location, also turned, paralleling the turn of the stockade. Although the cement marker was discovered here with some puzzlement during the opening days of the project, it was now no surprise to find that this ditch corner was exactly where the marker had been placed in 1921.

Fort Blue Mounds Revealed

The Fort Blue Mounds archaeological project excavated more than 1,500 square feet during the course of eight field seasons. Given the goals of the project, not all features were completely excavated once they were identified

FIGURE 3.17

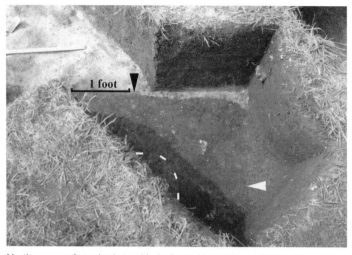

North corner of stockade trench, indicated by arrow and dotted line

and mapped, leaving these and the unexcavated part of the fort for future research (Figure 3.18). Sample excavations in the interior of the fort demonstrated that much remained preserved there and it, too, would provide opportunities for future investigation.

The project recovered thousands of artifacts and produced hundreds of maps, photographs, and records. Together with a careful comparison to historical records, all of this information contributed to the artist's conception of the fort site as it appeared in 1832. The rendering in Figure 3.19 shows a structure built in a familiar frontier military fort pattern, with two opposing blockhouses and a central building—a layout similar to those of several other Black Hawk War settlers' forts.

Archaeological excavations found that Fort Blue Mounds was about one-third the size indicated by eyewitnesses' accounts written many years after the fact. Built of oak logs, it formed a rectangular enclosure with walls fifty-five feet and forty-five feet in length, with the corners oriented to the cardinal directions. A defensive ditch paralleled the stockade. Gaps in the stockade and defensive ditch describe the location of blockhouses made of horizontal logs at the east and west corners, which projected out from the fort and allowed for a view of the adjacent walls.

FIGURE 3.18

FIGURE 3.18

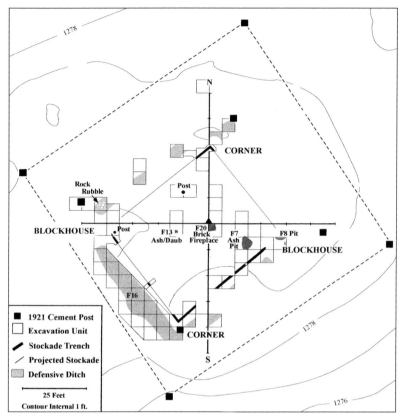

Final archaeological map of the Fort Blue Mounds site

Some details are lacking as yet, such as the size the central building, the location of an entrance or entrances, and the exact sizes of the blockhouses. Given the size of the fort, there would have been no room for wagons or livestock, so it is unlikely that it had a large gate. More likely an entrance or entrances would have been narrow gaps in the stockade, perhaps next to one or both of the blockhouses, as the excavation at the eastern blockhouse area suggests. The size of the blockhouses at Fort Blue Mounds could not be determined by excavations, but the gaps in the stockade could have accommodated the corners of the structures, twenty feet or longer, described in the historical accounts.

FIGURE 3.19

Artist's conception of Fort Blue Mounds, based on archaeological and
historical information

Drawing by Mark Heinrichs, based on a preliminary sketch by Mike Thorson

Some artifacts, like the 1837 coin and the English Texian Campaigne
plate made after 1848, verify that the fort site was reoccupied by miners after
the war, and there is evidence that the simple and quickly built blockhouses
were refurbished as more substantial living quarters between 1832 and 1850.
As mining resumed at the site after the war, the structures most likely were
converted to proper cabins, and the miners moved to the site to work at
Brigham's diggings.

Descriptions and analyses of the many artifacts found during the excavations further detail the history of Fort Blue Mounds. The stories of these
artifacts, which tell much about the people who lived there and life on the
Michigan Territory frontier, follow.

4

THE STORIES ARTIFACTS TELL

CAREFUL DIGGING EXPOSED stockade walls and other remains of Fort Blue Mounds, unearthing many thousands of mostly broken artifacts. Some of the artifacts came from features that could be attributed to one period of occupation or another. Most of the artifacts, however, either came from the plow zone, where they were displaced from their original location, or they were redeposited in filled defensive ditches. These artifacts nevertheless contribute to the reconstruction of life at the site and the fort itself. The archaeological volunteers found each discovery exciting, however humble.

Aside from being associated with dramatic historic events, the material culture of the people of Fort Blue Mounds is interesting and important since the 1830s to 1850s were a time of technological change and innovation associated with the beginnings of the Industrial Revolution. Artifacts from archaeological sites provide information on how fast these changes spread, as well as how these changes were incorporated into people's lives—choices based on economic, social, and even ethnic patterns. This was also a time of cultural change. Settlers from the East and new waves of immigrants adapted to new surroundings and new ways of life, adding their own elements to the emerging American culture. Numerous other nineteenth-century sites have been examined throughout the Midwest, including two Black Hawk War settlers' fortifications—the Apple River Fort at Elizabeth and Beggs's Fort or Fort Walker at Plainfield, both in Illinois—allowing for comparisons and identification of broad patterns in material culture.[1]

Personally, a few objects in particular helped me envision the people behind the artifacts. One was the shovel or pick part found in the stockade trench, broken by a frantic fort builder as he hit hard bedrock near the surface, described in chapter 3. One can well image the profanities uttered in the moment by that hard-bitten frontiersman. Other telling objects are clay marbles and a hand-carved bone domino tile, likely used to while away stressful times at the fort (Figure 4.1). The game of marbles was, as it is today, played by children. The marbles conjure up images of children playing in a corner of the fort or in a blockhouse, surrounded by visibly frightened adults busy with urgent tasks or nervously awaiting an Indian attack. The domino piece is similar to one found during excavations of the Second Fort Crawford (occupied 1829–1856) at Prairie du Chien, which shows the game's popularity at the time.[2]

The personal item we recovered in the area of the eastern blockhouse at the beginning of the field investigations in 1991 was also of interest to me: an initialed sealing wax stamp attached to a long metal chain, like that of a watch chain. Considered stylish for men at the time the fort was constructed, these seal fobs undoubtedly conferred some status on the owner. The stamp itself was apparently made of hard wax encased in a white metal oval. Unfortunately, the brittle stamp part dried out quickly after it was removed from the ground, cracking before it could be conserved. This was a rare—if not singular—find. The raised letter *J* on the stamp identifies the owner and was probably the initial of a surname of one of the men living at or visiting the fort site.

Given the comings and goings of many people during the war and the use of the site by miners after the war, we will never know with certainty to

FIGURE 4.1

½ inch

Clay marble and domino piece

Wisconsin Historical Society collections

whom the stamp belonged. But, provocatively, the muster roll of the Blue Mounds militia mentions only one name starting with that letter: Johnson, or Esau Johnson, the same man who left behind the memoirs that so greatly emphasized and exaggerated his role in the events of Fort Blue Mounds and the Black Hawk War. Johnson later recounted that he and his family had occupied one of the blockhouses during the war and also noted that he returned to live at the fort for a short time immediately after.[3] Johnson may have secured the place in history he greatly desired through the loss of a monogrammed and much-treasured item that is a dramatic and rare archaeological find.

The following describes a selection of other key artifacts that tell us much about the history of the site and the lives of those who lived there. A complete inventory is given under appendix III.

The Guns of Blue Mounds and the Black Hawk War

As would be expected from a fortification, a major category of artifacts is directly related to weapons and ammunition. Among these artifacts are lead balls, the remains of molds from the manufacture of lead balls, gunflints, and one lead gunflint cap or grip used to secure a flint into the jaws of the gun cock. A number of percussion caps, commonly used to fire weapons after about 1840, are attributed to later use of the site.

As discussed earlier, the Blue Mounds settler-miners had few weapons before the Black Hawk War began, a situation common to other mining and farming communities that constructed fortifications and formed militia. According to Esau Johnson, the men (the muster roll lists forty-two) had only a few shotguns, rifles, and pistols among them, and repeated requests to military authorities for muskets went unheeded. The fort never received the requested muskets, and Johnson explained that they were finally forced to make a trip up to Fort Winnebago to get worn-out army surplus weapons.[4]

The arms of the period were mainly muzzle-loaded flintlocks. When fired, a gunflint struck a metal frizzen, producing sparks that ignited gunpowder in a pan, which in turn ignited gunpowder through a hole in the barrel (Figure 4.2). The explosion threw a lead ball or balls that had been packed into the barrel with the gunpowder with a ramrod. The military employed paper cartridges loaded with gunpowder, a musket ball, and several pieces of shot. Soldiers would rip open the cartridge and pour the contents down the barrel.

A variety of flintlock rifles, muskets, and pistols used in the war were manufactured for either military or public use. Brigham identified the rifle taken by Indians as a "U.S. Yauger." A rifle has spiral grooves cut into the barrel to add spin to the projectile, while a musket has a smooth bore; both were used at the time. The "Yauger," or Yager, was the generic term for a short rifle, derived from the German-made Jager. Robert Braun of the Old Lead Mine Region Historical Society, an expert on Black Hawk War arms, suspects that the weapon is a .54-caliber 1803 pattern Harpers Ferry Rifle used during the War of 1812. His research indicates that quantities of these rifles came into the lead-mining district after the Winnebago Uprising of 1827 for use by the militias.[5]

Esau Johnson said that the fort defenders acquired a blunderbuss—a fowling piece—from Galena, as well as a 6 pounder, a field cannon that threw a six-pound ball. The records of the US military quartermaster at Fort Jackson at Mineral Point, however, show a swivel gun signed out to the

FIGURE 4.2

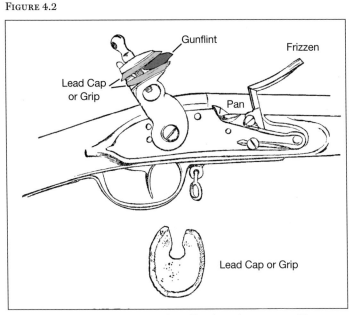

Flintlock gun mechanism and drawing of lead patch or cap used to secure gunflint

After Fig. 42 in *Guns on the Early Frontiers*, by Carl P. Russell (University of California Press, 1957)

FIGURE 4.3

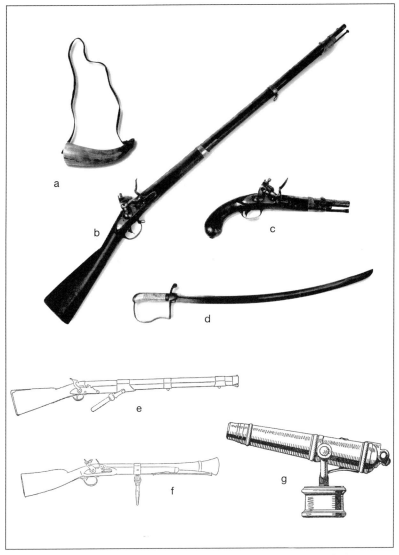

Some weapons of the Black Hawk War: a) Colonel Henry Dodge's powder horn, b) US Pattern 1816 Springfield flintlock rifle marked with the date 1832, c) example of an early nineteenth-century flintlock pistol, d) sword used by militia company captain John Roundtree of Platteville. Examples of period swivel guns: e) rifle, f) blunderbuss, and g) small cannon

a) WHS Museum 1947.851, b) WHS Museum 1947.1720, c) WHS Museum R204, d) WHS Museum 1947.750, e–g) From Figs. 46 and 48 in *Guns on the Early Frontiers*, by Carl P. Russell (University of California Press, 1957)

"Mound Fort." Either the blunderbuss or the cannon could have been that swivel, since both were commonly mounted on swivels (Figures 4.3f and g). Also, according to Johnson, he and Brigham obtained 150 "worn out" muskets from Fort Winnebago that had to be repaired, providing "three to every man."[6] The models are not given, and the number is almost certainly a great exaggeration. The only gun parts found at Fort Blue Mounds are gunflints and a broken lead gunflint patch or grip, and the sizes of musket balls found so far at the site do not support the presence of a large number of military-issue arms, either old or new.

At the time of the Black Hawk War, the military generally used a large-bore .69-caliber musket, which the US military issued in many models between 1795 and 1840. The US military supplied militias a great many muskets during the Black Hawk War, and these may have been the pattern 1795 Springfield used during the War of 1812 or either of the Springfield patterns 1812 or 1816 (Figure 4.3b).[7] In mid-June 1832, Fort Jackson at Mineral Point had several hundred muskets for militia use in the Michigan Territory.[8]

Judging from the sizes of musket balls discovered at the Fort Blue Mounds site, only a few of these large-bore weapons reached the fort—and perhaps were only found in the hands of mounted rangers assigned to the fort at various times or members of the US military itself when troops joined the militia at Blue Mounds in July 1832 after the Battle of Wisconsin Heights. The presence of some US issue arms and supplies is confirmed by other evidence, but analysis of lead artifacts also shows that people of the fort were making much of their own ammunition in the form of small shot, to be used in shotguns and perhaps the swivel gun, as well as some musket balls.

Lead and Lead Balls

Over the course of our archaeological project, we recovered a large sample (107) of lead balls of various sizes, primarily from the interior of the fort where they had been dropped and lost (Figure 4.4a). These ranged in size from a small .25 shot to a large .65 musket ball, but the vast majority were in the range of what is called buckshot and still used in shotguns (Figure 4.4b). Only one of these balls had been flattened, an indication that it had been fired. The measurements or calibers in this graph are given in tenths of an inch. Those lead balls measuring less than .45 are classified as shot, while larger diameters are referred to as a musket ball.[9]

FIGURE 4.4B

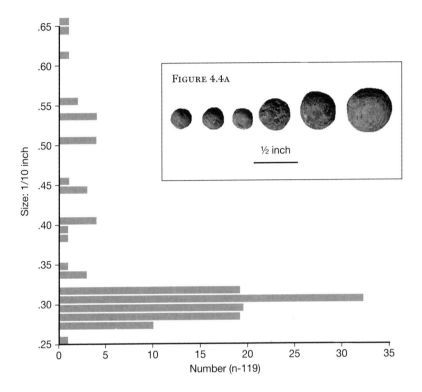

Graph showing the sizes of shot and musket balls found at the fort site. Inset, shot and musket balls.

Except for two large-caliber musket balls, the balls were cast in two-piece molds, as indicated by mold seams on the balls. Common objects found at the fort's interior were unprocessed lead (galena), chunks of melted lead waste, cut pieces of melted lead, and pieces of lead from the mold castings called sprue (Figure 4.5). The lead was melted in a small, circular iron pan and then poured into molds or cut up into pieces to be saved for later remelting and casting. Shot was cast in gang molds, which produced a thin lead rod with many balls attached. When needed, the shot would be snapped off the rod, thereby minimizing accidental loss of ammunition. All of the shot recovered at the site had flat spurs where the ball was attached to the lead sprue of the

FIGURE 4.5

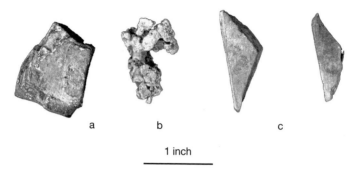

a   b   c

1 inch

Lead: a) unprocessed lead cube, or galena, b) lead waste created during the process of melting lead for shot and musket balls in molds, c) cut lead pieces

Wisconsin Historical Society collections

gang molds, as did one musket ball. Musket balls with just mold seams would have been made in individual molds.

We found shot throughout the excavated areas. By far, most of the shot from the site conforms to a size range commonly called buckshot, with the highest frequency at .30 inch in diameter. Two of these were found still attached to a gang mold. Two other smaller clusters of shot ranged between .38 and .40, and .43 and .45. The musket balls ranged in size from .45 to .64. Three other musket balls had been malformed in production and one ball had human teeth marks. Chewed musket balls are an occasional find on military and other sites, and are generally interpreted as either the result of nervous behavior or an indication of a gunman having held a spare ball in his mouth for reloading. Chewing could also round out malformed balls so they fit into the gun barrel.

Only two balls would fit the US military–issue large-bore muskets. Accounting for windage—the .04 space needed to fit the ball in the barrel— the .64 and .65 would fit the .69-caliber muskets used by the military. One of these balls came from the floor of the western blockhouse. The "buck and ball" paper cartridges used for these weapons contained .63 ball, three .31 shot, and powder, although some slight variation in sizes would be expected.[10] Archaeological excavations at Second Fort Crawford at Prairie du Chien produced many balls between .64 and .66, along with some shot in the appropriate cartridge range.[11]

The other musket balls would fit a variety of military and civilian weapons, including pistols. Brigham reports that one pistol (his) had been taken by Indians during the June 6 attack. Johnson said he owned two. The .50 and .52 inch balls would also have fit the .54-caliber Model 1803, including possibly Brigham's "Yauger." The most common musket balls are .54, a size likely used for a nonmilitary weapon.

The presence of pre-prepared buck and ball cartridges could feasibly account for the high number of shot in the .31 range at Fort Blue Mounds. As of mid-June 1832, Fort Jackson had 1,000 cartridges available for distribution to militia.[12] But the presence to date of only two appropriately sized balls and the high number of shot-mold sprue at the Fort Blue Mounds site strongly suggests that the shot was manufactured onsite rather than delivered in cartridges.

Gunflints and Gunflint Grip

Spent or lost gunflints are commonly found on archaeological sites of the period between the 1700s and 1840s. Gunflints fit into the jaws of a gun cock and ignite the gunpowder with sparks when the flint hits a metal frizzen. Settlers, soldiers, and Indians used fine flints imported from Europe both to fire their flintlock guns and to make fires. A fire-starting kit consisting of a steel "strike-a-light," or "fire steel," flint and tinder was a standard and necessary personal possession. One oval, handwrought object found at the site is typical of the size and form of a strike-a-light or fire steel, but one part is broken off (Figure 4.6). The surviving edge shows no sign of battering, which suggests it might have broken during manufacture or initial use because of a flaw in the steel.

In Europe, the ancient art of flint knapping had been revived with the invention of the flintlock in the early 1600s. Whereas, in America, the craft of making stone tools had diminished among Indian people by the 1800s. Despite the presence of appropriate

FIGURE 4.6

1 inch

Wrought-iron piece that is probably from a strike-a-light broken during manufacture

Wisconsin Historical Society collections

FIGURE 4.7

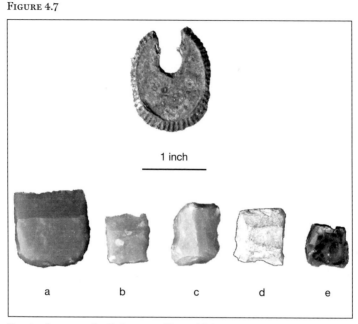

1 inch

a   b   c   d   e

Top, lead cap or grip. Bottom, gunflints: a) little-used honey-colored
French flint, b–c) worn French flints, d) white flint that had been burned or
exposed to heat, e) well-worn British black flint used with a strike-a-light

Wisconsin Historical Society collections

spark-producing rock, a domestic commercial industry never developed in
America probably due to a lack of the necessary expertise.

Most of the flints at Fort Blue Mounds (11 of 15) are honey-colored gunflints imported from France (Figure 4.7). Three flakes driven from French
flints during reshaping or use were also found. Two are black flints from the
Brandon flint manufacturing area in England, and two others—from Feature
16, the large defensive ditch filled with ash—had been burned white, making
it impossible to establish their origins. The presence of so many French gunflints suggests they were obtained from US Army supplies. The military pre-
ferred the high-grade French gunflints—a preference that may have been a
consequence of the Revolutionary War and the War of 1812, when British
arms and supplies obviously would not have been available to American
forces. Most of the gunflints (12 of 19) recovered from archaeological excavations at Second Fort Crawford are also French.[13]

The French flints at Blue Mounds are a wide range of sizes. One large unused flint shown in Figure 4.7 is for a large-bore musket such as the military .69 caliber. Two others with signs of minimal use are for smaller-bore arms.

French gunflints are occasionally found on other types of nineteenth-century sites, such as settlers' cabins, but most often the civilian population used black British gunflints. The British flints from Fort Blue Mounds show excessive use, suggesting they would have been used to start fires with a metal strike-a-light.

Another indication of at least some US military arms at Fort Blue Mounds is the presence of one lead gunflint cap or grip used to secure the flint in the jaws of the cock (Figure 4.7). Among civilians, such grips were commonly made of leather, but the military used lead since repeated firing during battle would heat the metal of the cock and cause the leather to burn. Lead caps or grips were used on muskets, pistols, and especially rifles. Archaeologists unearthed a number of lead patches similar to the one at Fort Blue Mounds at both the First and the Second Fort Crawford.[14]

Percussion Caps

Invented in 1807, the brass percussion cap carried a small charge of gunpowder and fit over the end of the gun cock (Figure 4.8), thereby eliminating the

FIGURE 4.8

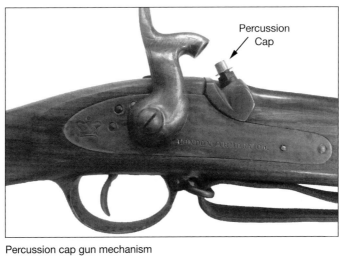

Percussion
Cap

Percussion cap gun mechanism

need for a gunflint. In the 1830s, percussion cap weapons began to replace flintlocks in North America, and often the old weapons were simply converted with the new technology. In 1840 the US military adopted percussion-cap weapons, and these were used during the American Civil War.[15] A total of twenty-five caps were recovered at Fort Blue Mounds, some of them fragmentary. Most are believed to represent postwar activities, such as occasional hunting. However, discoveries at the Apple River Fort site suggest that its occupants had one percussion-cap weapon during the Black Hawk War, so it is possible that such a weapon was also at Fort Blue Mounds at the same time.[16]

Frontier Dishware and Pottery

Ceramic or pottery vessels constitute a particularly useful class of artifacts for the study of archaeological sites of the nineteenth century since they were a common possession with frequent style changes, which provide a helpful means of dating sites. Oftentimes the stamps of ceramic makers noting the places and dates of manufacture are on the bottom of a vessel. The various types of ceramics also provide insight into activities and the socioeconomic status of individuals, sites, and communities. Previous historical and archaeological studies have established the time ranges and other information of various ceramic styles used in North America and on the midwestern frontier, which facilitates analysis of artifacts from Fort Blue Mounds and similar sites.[17]

Our excavation produced nearly 1,600 pieces, most of which were too small to identify owing to years of breakage by plowing. Some were burned, and these came mainly from the burned debris in the southwest ditch, Feature 16; an ash pit next to the eastern blockhouse, Feature 7; and a hearth or forge area, Feature 20, in the interior of the fort.

Many, though, could be easily identified and are from more than thirty ceramic vessels. These are mainly colorfully decorated English-produced tableware, such as plates and cups, and, interestingly, components to fancy tea sets, as well as a small number of utilitarian vessels, such as mixing bowls, jugs, and storage containers, that were made in the United States (Figure 4.9). England was a large center of pottery production, and a wide variety of up-to-date English wares are commonly found on nineteenth-century sites throughout North America, including frontier areas. This attests to both the importance of these objects as symbols of civilization as well as the efficiency

FIGURE 4.9

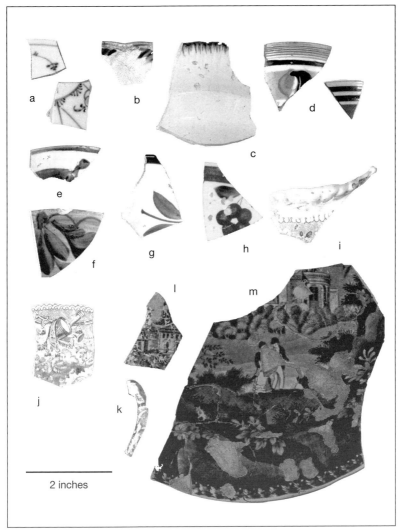

2 inches

Examples of decorated ceramic sherds: a) porcelain cup or bowl, b) green edge decorated or painted plate, c) blue edge decorated or painted plate, d) banded slipware or annular ware bowls, e–g) hand-painted blue floral bowls, h) hand-painted polychrome floral bowl, i) brown transferprint sugar bowl, j) brown transferprint Texian Campaigne series plate, k) blue transferprint handle to teacup, teapot, or bowl, l) blue transferprint plate, m) cobalt blue transferprint Villa in the Regent's Park, London pattern plate

of the shipping and transportation networks of the time. Americans continued to buy English pottery for their tables until late in the nineteenth century, when American potteries proliferated, often imitating English wares that carried a connotation of quality.

Surprisingly, components to tea sets are among the most common ceramics found on the frontier. The English and European custom of taking tea as a virtual ritual attained great importance to the colonists of the East Coast, and the common use of tea sets on the frontier suggests that this custom accompanied those settlers as they migrated west. Tea itself, however, became less important. Robert Mazrim, who made an extensive study of both the records of local merchants in Illinois and the remains of tea sets at many archaeological sites there, found that, while the possession of English tea sets remained important links to civilization, by the 1830s, rural settlers mostly drank coffee. He notes: "If the tea ceremony itself was fading within rural contexts, the archaeological record makes clear that the tradition of shopping for tea equipment remained strong well into the fourth decade of the [nineteenth] century."[18] The store records of Ebenezer Brigham at Blue Mounds show orders for both coffee and tea.

Most of the ceramic styles at Fort Blue Mounds are common to the period 1832–1850 and include styles that would be expected to have been in use at the time of the Black Hawk War. One vessel is of a type manufactured and used prior to this time. Several vessels bear English maker's marks, and one of these, along with its ornate decoration, confirms that the fort site continued to be used long after the Black Hawk War.

Undecorated

Five vessels discovered at the Fort Blue Mounds site are undecorated. One plate, found in the defensive ditch fill, is creamware, a form of fine earthenware that has a yellowish or cream-colored paste and a clear lead glaze produced from circa 1760 until the 1820s. An undecorated creamware plate was discovered at the Apple River Fort excavations, where it is interpreted as dating to a brief earlier use of the site area.[19] The presence of a similar plate at Blue Mounds could suggest the same period and use, but it is also possible that some vessels were simply left from earlier times and places and somehow kept undamaged by the settlers. Four plain vessels are whiteware, so named because of their distinctive white color. Whiteware began appearing about

1830 and dominated refined earthenware, such as dishware and tea sets, until about 1850, when the whiteware was replaced by a heavier-bodied and somewhat grayer ware called ironstone. The whiteware at Blue Mounds is in the form of three plates and a cup. Two of the plates came from Feature 16, along with other pottery described below.

Utilitarian Vessels

While Americans bought dishware and tea sets from England, domestic potteries for the manufacture of coarse earthenware utilitarian vessels such as jugs, crocks, and kitchen bowls developed during colonial times.[24] Utilitarian vessels found at the site are redware, stoneware, and yellowware. Redware is a soft, red-pasted earthenware commonly used for pans, bowls, jugs, and jars. All twenty-four redware fragments from the site have orange-yellow glaze on the exterior. Two of the pieces are to a base of a jug with out-curving sides characteristic of similar vessels from the period. Jugs on the frontier often carried whiskey, a substance that would not have been foreign to the male-dominated lead-mining community. Most of the glazed redware sherds were found adjacent to the western blockhouse either in the southwest defensive ditch, Feature 16, or nearby in the west end of the northeast defensive ditch, Feature 18.

Stoneware is a durable, vitrified ware and all sherds are gray with a dark-brown slipped interior. The sherds, probably all from crocks, were found mainly in the eastern half of the site and mainly in plow-zone contexts. Two stoneware sherds were recovered from the stockade line and defensive ditch. A small number of sherds found at the site appear to be yellowware, a type of earthenware that has yellow or buff-colored paste and a clear glaze that brings out the yellow. Often used for mixing bowls, yellowware was made by North American potters, first in the East in the 1830s and then by midwestern potteries after 1850. Most of the sherds at the Fort Blue Mounds site (11 of 15) are from a single bowl, decorated with white bands, found at the interior of the fort.

Decorated

Villa in the Regent's Park, London Plate

Large fragments of decorated pearlware also came from Feature 16 and could well have graced the table of Ebenezer Brigham and then been brought to the fort at the time of the war (see chapter 2). Figure 4.10 shows a complete plate identical to the fragments found at the site. It has a beautiful pattern in cobalt blue applied by a process called transferprinting, and it is identified on the back mark as *Villa in the Regent's Park, London*. Potters introduced the transferprint process in the late eighteenth century. This process entailed the engraving of an image on a copper plate onto which colored inks were applied. The image was then transferred to a paper and placed on an undecorated ceramic piece that was then glazed and fired. The copper image could be reused, allowing for mass production. In this case, the pattern scene appears on pearlware that has a distinctive bluish cast as a result of using cobalt in the glaze—a process used in England until the early 1830s, when whiter ware became common.

Along with the pattern name, an impressed maker's mark identifies the plate as a product of Adams Company of Staffordshire, England, and the central American eagle indicates that it was made for the American market.[20] In a remarkable coincidence, during the archaeological work at Fort Blue Mounds, the Massachusetts Historical Commission chose an identical plate,

FIGURE 4.10

a b c

Three of the colorful plates represented by sherds at the Fort Blue Mounds site: a) blue edge decorated or painted plate, b) brown transferprint Texian Campaigne series plate, c) cobalt blue transferprint Villa in the Regent's Park, London pattern plate found in Boston, for a poster promoting Massachusetts Archaeology Month for 1996. This not only rapidly identified our plate but also illustrates that the people of a small, remote western frontier settlement had access to the same fancy English dishware as people living in urban and cosmopolitan Boston.

Other Transferprints

Other smaller sherds came from transferprinted vessels in blue, brown, red, black, and lavender (Figure 4.9). Blue transferprints included several sherds with deep blues similar to the above mentioned pearlware, but most are a lighter blue typically found on later whiteware; the latter were found throughout the excavated areas of the site. Most of a broken plate came from the same area of Feature 16 as the pearlware plate described above and seems to have been a part of the same dumping. The north part of the southwest defensive ditch produced the handle of a blue transferprinted teacup or small bowl.

Brown transferprinted vessels consisted of at least two plates, one plate or saucer, a sugar bowl, and parts of a pitcher or teapot. All were found within the walls of the fort proper. One concentration of brown sherds came from the same place where a brick hearth or forge, Feature 20, was discovered. Some burned brown sherds were found in Feature 7, the ash pit next to the eastern blockhouse, but others in this feature are from a brown transferprint plate with a militaristic scene and maker's mark on the back that reads in part *Texian Campaigne* (Figures 4.9 and 4.10). Several Staffordshire, England, potteries appealed to the American market by producing Texian Campaigne patterns between the late 1830s and 1850s portraying fanciful scenes of the 1835–1836 Texas war of independence from Mexico and especially the Mexican-American War of 1846–1848.[21] English potters produced a number of different patterns in this series and these were imported in great quantities to the United States. The fragments from the Fort Blue Mounds site, however, were too small to identify the specific pattern. The brown transferprint plate dates the use of Feature 7 to late in the history of the site and shows that the miners lived here after the late 1830s.

Edge Decorated

The most common type of plate and platter decorations of the period are molded edges, often called a feather edge, painted in blue or green (Figures 4.9 and 4.10).[22] Green is mostly common on pearlware produced until the early 1830s, while blue is common on later whiteware and ironstone. These edge decorated ceramics were the least expensive of the decorated ware, and they are the most common type of plate found at Blue Mounds. Rim pieces are from eight different vessels, presumably plates. Three of the vessels represented are green edged and five are blue edged.

Hand Painted

Other more elaborately decorated vessels discovered at the site, also parts of tea sets, are painted with floral designs: broad designs in reds, oranges, and greens or just shades of blue and sprigs of green with black-lined stems (Figures 4.9e–h). These also show a transition of styles, since some of the broad florals on pearlware and the sprigs on whiteware became common after 1830. Both are typical of archaeological ceramic assemblages of the region. Defensive ditch Feature 16, which produced the pearlware Villa in the Regent's Park, London plate, also produced a burned bowl with a broad blue floral design typical of pearlware, while sherds from the later sprig design came from the Feature 7 ash pit along with the Texian Campaigne plate made after 1848.

Banded Decorations

Pottery with colored bands was also mass-produced in England and imported to America during the early nineteenth century. This type of pottery is variously referred to as dipped, annular, or slip ware. This decoration type was most commonly used on hollow vessel forms such as bowls and was made by applying different colors of slip while the vessel was turned on a lathe.

These banded designs appear on a number of sherds discovered at the site, but the most unusual is a "cat's eye" motif made by a multichamber slip cup that delivered several colors simultaneously by means of quills attached to the cup (Figure 4.9d).[23] This design is many times accompanied with a "wormed," or cable, element made in the same fashion. The impressed design around the rim on both of the Fort Blue Mounds sherds and the sample vessel were made by machine.

Utensils

Period kitchen and table utensils discovered at the site consisted of metal spoons, knives, and two-tined forks (Figure 4.11). The knives and forks had

FIGURE 4.11

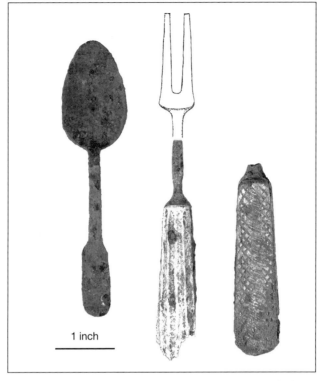

1 inch

Utensils: metal spoon, fluted bone fork handle, crosshatch-incised
bone handle from a fork or knife

Wisconsin Historical Society collections

wood, bone, or deer antler handles. The utensils of Fort Blue Mounds are
fragmentary and found in the areas of the two blockhouses, with most in and
around the eastern concentration of domestic debris. This area also produced
the bowl to a mixing spoon, a handle to a metal teaspoon, an antler knife
handle, a two-tined fork, and a decorated bone fork or knife handle. Another
bone fork handle came from the filled-in defensive ditch just north of the
western blockhouse.

Bottles

Glass bottles found at the site held four types of liquids: whiskey, wine, medicine, and perfume (Figure 4.12). At least ten glass bottles are represented,

mostly by colored shards. During the nineteenth century, bottles were blown in molds with the tops and lips formed by special tools, so these are easy to distinguish from modern styles mass-produced by machines.

Given the dominance of males at Fort Blue Mounds, including many single miners, it is not surprising that bottles containing alcohol are

FIGURE 4.12

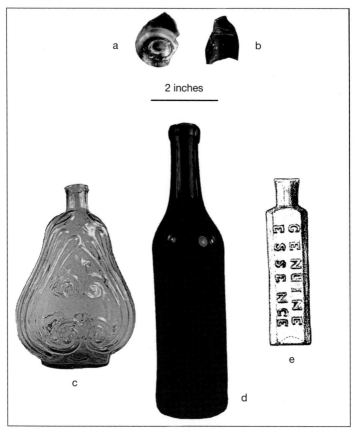

All bottles at the site were found in the form of shards similar to the small, cylindrical bottle base and lip fragment from a dark-green wine bottle shown as a) and b). The full bottles shown are examples of the major vessels represented by fragments at the site: c) scroll-decorated whiskey flask, d) dark wine bottle, e) Essence of Peppermint bottle

a) and b) Wisconsin Historical Society collections; e) Drawing from "The Marina Site" by Robert A. Birmingham and Robert Salzer, report on file, Division of Historic Preservation, Wisconsin Historical Society, 1984

common at the site. We found fragments of two dark-green wine bottles; the large base of one was discovered deep in the defensive ditch at the south corner of the fort. Whiskey in the 1830s came in a variety of decorative glass whiskey flasks molded into scroll patterns or featuring the busts of historical people such as presidents. Excavations at the Apple River Fort site produced flask fragments believed to bear the likeness of John Quincy Adams,[25] while Blue Mounds shards are from two scroll-pattern flasks like that shown in Figure 4.12.

Patent medicine was commonly used on the frontier, a place with few doctors. A wide variety of cure-alls came in glass bottles, and the magic ingredient in many was a good dose of alcohol. One commonly used elixir was called Essence of Peppermint, and fragments of two such bottles were found during the Fort Blue Mounds excavations. The broken shards to three small, delicate perfume bottles tell of the presence of women at the site, and they were mostly located in the area of the eastern blockhouse along with domestic debris.

Other Containers

One early type of tin food can was found crushed in the defensive ditch at the south corner of the site. Foods in tin cans were first produced in England in 1810 but were not commonly available until much later. Pieces of a larger tin container were found elsewhere in the ditch. One large kettle handle and a broken rim to a pan—both made of wrought iron—were found, as were parts of barrel hoops (Figure 4.13). The thick iron kettle and pan were probably fractured as a result of repeated intense heating, which would have made the metal brittle.

FIGURE 4.13

1 inch

Handle from a large wrought-iron kettle

Wisconsin Historical Society collections

Possible Items from the Indian Trade

Three small glass necklace beads common to the early nineteenth century were all found in the defensive ditch fill next to the eastern blockhouse (Figure 4.14). These are blue tubular, black barrel-shaped, and blue faceted beads

FIGURE 4.14

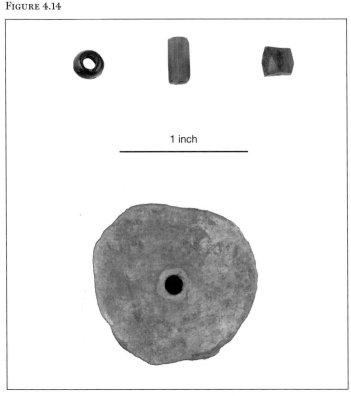

1 inch

Top, glass beads. Bottom, back part of a bale seal.

often referred to as Russian blue. Such beads are found on homesteads and farmsteads of American settlers,[26] but they were mainly an item of trade with Native Americans. Significantly, the back of a pronged lead-bale seal used to secure packs of pelts came from the same area. Both Ebenezer Brigham and Edward Beouchard engaged in the trade for fur with the Ho-Chunk. It is feasible that these items are unrelated and only coincidentally found in the same area of fill. But it is entirely possible that trade goods and pelts were brought to the fort and kept in the western blockhouse—the one thought to have been Brigham's—for safekeeping, for trading, or for gifting the Ho-Chunk after the war had started. The Ho-Chunk came to the fort several times during this period, according to the historical record.

Personal Garments

The discovery of clothing would be rare on any archaeological site, but there does exist a rich historical record. Figure 4.15 shows how settlers of the lead-mining region would have dressed between 1830 and 1850. Juliette Kinzie, the wife of Indian agent John Kinzie, recounts a trip through the lead-mining region in 1831, traveling from Fort Winnebago to Fort Dearborn at Chicago, and she describes the rather rough appearance and character of the people living there. Resting at Hamilton's diggings at modern-day Wiota, Wisconsin, she describes the miners of that place as: "The roughest-looking set of men I ever beheld, and their language was uncouth as their persons. They wore hunting-shirts, trowsers, and moccasins of deer-skin, the former being ornamented at the seams with a fringe of the same, while a colored belt around the waist, in which was stuck a large hunting-knife, gave each the appearance of a brigand."[27]

Hamilton's housekeeper wore a "tidy calico dress and a shabby black silk cap trimmed with still shabbier lace."[28] In contrast to the roughness of the miners, Kinzie characterizes the head of the settlement, William "Billy" Stephen Hamilton, son of the famous Secretary of the Treasury Alexander Hamilton, as polite, amusing, and highly literate.

Clothing-related items found at the site by archaeologists consist of a wide variety of buttons, snaps, and buckles, as well as three thimbles and a pin used for sewing. Buttons of various sizes were made from bone (5), shell (2), brass (5), and ferrous metal (11), and include a button from a US military uniform (Figure 4.15). Many brass buttons of the time came from English button factories, especially in Birmingham, England, while shell and bone buttons were produced domestically. One brass button bore a maker's stamp on the reverse with the words *GILT* and *TOPS* interspersed with stars. Another brass button found at the site is a two-piece decorative button, likely from a woman's garment, featuring a flower and encircling decoration on the front and a maker's mark—*EADRICK EXTRA*—on the reverse.

The most interesting button is the brass US military button from the fill of the defensive ditch in the west corner of the fort site. It bears a prominent *US* with an eagle above and an oval cartouche below. On the reverse are the words *United States,* standing for the United States Button Company of Connecticut. Archaeological excavations produced identical buttons at Second Fort Crawford, and they are identified as being from a "great coat"—a

FIGURE 4.15

Top, members of the Old Lead Mine Region Historical Society model clothing of the Black Hawk War era in Michigan Territory. Bottom, buttons recovered from the Fort Blue Mounds site: a) bone, b–c) plain brass, d) metal with floral decoration, e) brass US military coat button. Fragments of shell buttons were also found.

Top, photos by Robert and Mary Braun; bottom, Wisconsin Historical Society collections

cold-weather coat with a short cape.[29] Federal troops under the command of General Atkinson spent several days at Blue Mounds just after the Battle of Wisconsin Heights on July 21, and this is one possible explanation for the presence of the button at the site. While a heavy coat would have been unnecessary during that warm summer, the army campaign had started back in the spring.

Tobacco Pipes

Just about every man of the period carried a long-stemmed white clay pipe and a tobacco pouch for a quick smoke between activities (Figure 4.16). Fragments of white clay tobacco pipes are common to nineteenth-century sites of all types throughout North America and attest to widespread tobacco use and the availability of pipes, despite the fact that they came from England, Scotland, and other European counties. Some were plain, but many styles had bowls and stems decorated with various molded designs. Often the vessels bear maker's marks, enabling researchers to trace the country of origin and time of manufacture.

At the Blue Mounds site, we discovered fragments of at least ten different pipes in seven styles or types. The most common are ribbed or fluted designs that are found on many sites occupied during the second quarter of the nineteenth century. For example, archaeologists found the two styles shown in Figures 4.16a and 4.16b at the Apple River Fort and the style in Figure 4.16c at Second Fort Crawford.[30] Stem fragments from the pipes are plain, or they are decorated with a raised line-and-dot pattern or raised horizontal lines. One decorated stem section bore a line-and-dot pattern along partially readable words—*OER*[or B]*EL*—on one side and—*F . . . BUC . . .*—on the other.

One rare porcelain tobacco pipe bowl type found at the site is represented by a single fragment of a long white bowl decorated with a brown band. A similar piece was discovered at Second Fort Crawford and thought to be of German origin.[31] German immigrants came to this region with other early settlers and subsequently flooded into the state during later waves of immigration. German surnames are common today in the Blue Mounds area.

Finally, fragments of short, unglazed elbow pipe, reminiscent of Native American styles, were found in the fill of the ditch next to the blockhouse in the same area as the glass beads and the partial bale seal. Lines are incised at the bottom of the bowl. Examination of the finely molded interior indicates that it was mold-made like similarly formed pipes of American manufacture. Americans had produced pipes of this type, smoked through a reed, since colonial times.[32]

Coin

The only monetary treasure is a silver 1837 half dime, a precursor of the modern nickel, found in the defensive ditch (Figure 3.15). This is another object that indicates use of the site after the 1832 war. Both American and foreign coinage bought goods and services on the frontier. Even the soldiers of Second Fort Crawford used some Mexican coins,[33] and the people of the lead-mining district and other places sometimes cut up silver Mexican coins into eight wedges, referred to as "pieces of eight," to produce smaller denominations.

FIGURE 4.16

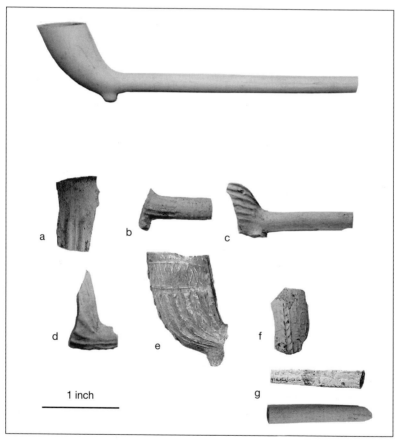

White clay pipes: Top, common form of a white clay pipe. Fragments from Fort Blue Mounds: a) bowl fragment with raised-line fluted style, b) stem-bowl juncture with fluted bowl and raised-line and dot-decorated stem, c) narrow raised-line bowl decoration, d) fluted bowl fragment, e) fluted bowl surmounted by crosshatching and with floral elements along the mold seam, f) bowl fragment with complex raised-line decoration, g) raised-line and dot-decorated pipe stem and plain pipe stem

Horses and Riding

Two broken fragments of stirrups discovered at the site are a brass strap loop
and a star-shaped spur (Figure 4.17).
These could well have come from the
boots of Dodge's mounted rangers. In
addition, excavations produced horseshoe nails and harness buckles, but
these could also have been deposited
by local farmers in more recent times.

Tools

As described earlier, the metal part of
a broken pick or shovel with a missing

FIGURE 4.17

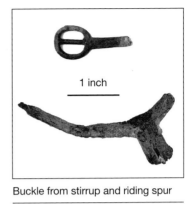

1 inch

Buckle from stirrup and riding spur

Wisconsin Historical Society collections

working end was found in the stockade trench. Another tool, found in an ash
dumping on top of the defensive ditch, is a broken and split wrought-iron
punch or chisel used in blacksmithing (Figure 4.18a). The ash found with this
piece is interpreted as a dumping from blacksmithing activities, specifically
the repair and manufacture of the heavy iron tools used in mining. Mining
is represented by what most likely is a knob for a fuel reservoir door on a
lenticular-shaped miner's lamp (Figure 4.18b).

Architectural Elements and Furnishings

We found remains of buildings in the form of chinking, whitewashed plaster, bricks, nails, and window glass. The original buildings were made of
horizontal logs and probably had bark-shingle roofs. Bricks comprised the
bases of fireboxes. Typically, clay chinking filled the spaces between logs
in log cabins, and the interior walls were plastered with clay. A dense scattering of hardened clay pieces, called daub, used as chinking and plaster
was found mainly around the blockhouses. Pieces of whitewashed plaster
were also found; some retain imprints of wood lath that would have been
attached to logs in the interior to form walls. The builders of the fort in 1832
would have had little time or need for much chinking and plastering since
the fort was meant to be temporary, therefore much of this material likely
reflects later modifications to the buildings as miners moved into them to
live. For the same reasons, window glass was unlikely to have been a part of

FIGURE 4.18

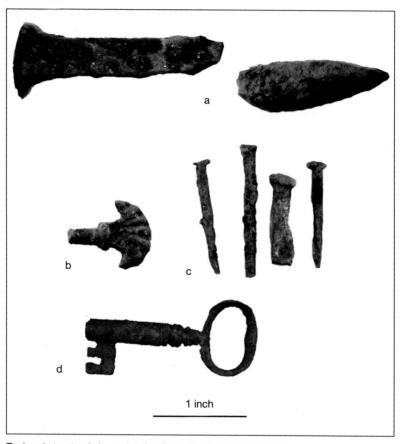

Tool and structural elements: a) split and broken iron punch or wedge, b) probable miner's lamp part, c) machine-cut nails, and d) padlock key

Wisconsin Historical Society collections

the 1832 fort buildings and, additionally, would had to have been ordered from distant places.

Nails

The fort site excavations yielded 113 intact nails and many others that were fragmentary or damaged, reflecting technical innovations in how nails were made (Figure 4.18c). Before 1830, blacksmiths hand-made iron nails at their forges. After 1830, machines mass-produced nails cut from sheets of metal iron, which greatly increased production and led to a building revolution.[34] Both types were found among the archaeological deposits, with machine-cut nails in the majority. Both the 11 intact wrought nails and 102 machine-cut nails share a similar size range of 1 inch to 3 inches (10d pennyweight) in length, with more than 60 percent of both types measuring 1¼ inch or less. These small nails would have been used in construction for flooring, roofing, and lath, or in the construction of boxes and barrels. The paucity of larger sizes reflects the fact that the fort buildings were of horizontal log construction rather than composed of planks. The lack of sawmills in the area at the time meant that planks would have been hard to acquire and so planks, as well as logs, had to be hand hewn. It is suspected that most of the nails were used when the buildings were refurbished as cabins, a theory supported by the larger number of machine-cut nails. One hand-wrought spike was likely used to fasten horizontal logs together at the corner of a building during the original construction in 1832. Eight modern wire nails from the plow zone are from more recent use.

Furniture Parts

Feature 16 produced a padlock key (Figure 4.18d) and six upholstery tacks, used to fasten fabric and leather to furniture and as decoration on trunks and other objects, were found scattered at various places.

Frontier Food

The people of the fort, and those who followed, deposited garbage with food remains in the form of animal bone and teeth. During the war, however, the settlers ran short of food and pleas were made to Dodge not only for guns but for provisions as well. Along with historical records, several thousand fragmentary skeletal elements found during excavations at Fort Blue Mounds provide a picture of the frontier diet in the oak savanna and prairies of south-central Wisconsin between 1832 and 1850. This was a frontier pattern of subsistence focusing on a rather narrow range of domesticated and wild animals, with supplementary foods grown in gardens or purchased from regional markets. Brigham's account books show that he sold pork, potatoes, coffee, and tea from his store.[35]

Small cultivated fields in the vicinity of Brigham's establishment are shown on the 1833 public land survey plat,[36] and today the Brigham farm (established in 1828) claims to be the oldest continually operating farm in Wisconsin. Esau Johnson said that at the time of the June 6 killing at Fort Blue Mounds, he continued to sow oats at this field and his wife was still tending a garden more than a mile and half away from the fort.[37] He and his wife were on their way to the field and the garden at the time of the attack on Aubrey and Smith. Such trips probably were made under heavy surveillance after these men were killed.

As with other archaeological assemblages, the animal remains from the fort are fragments and experts could identify only some by species. However, meticulous examination of more than 4,000 bones and teeth unearthed at the site—many with butchering marks—revealed that pig and deer supplied the bulk of the meat, along with some cattle, chicken, rabbit, and wild birds such as grouse and the now-extinct passenger pigeon (Table 1). Larger mammals make up most of the unidentified remains. There were also remains of a rodent and a fish.

TABLE 1

Identified Animal Bone from the Fort Blue Mounds Site, 1832 to circa 1850

Animal	Number of elements	Minimum # of individuals
Pig	127 (7 burned)	3 adults, 2 juveniles
Deer	106 (2 burned)	3 adults, 1 juvenile
Cattle	16 (2 burned)	1 adult, 1 juvenile
Ruffed grouse	4	1 adult
Cottontail rabbit	1	1 adult
Chicken	1	1 adult
Passenger pigeon	1	1 adult
Fish	1	
Vole*	1	
Horse* †	1	

*Not considered a food item
†One unbutchered horse bone from near the surface of the site is probably not related to the fort.

Pig remains were common at the site, and among them are a substantial number of head elements that include long tusks, the extended incisors of the animal. When confined, the sharp, dangerous tusks are generally cut to prevent injury to humans and other animals. The presence of tusks indicates that the pigs roamed freely and untended until the time of butchering. Pork was an important feature of the diet throughout the midwestern frontier but particularly so in this region, as also indicated by animal bone at the Apple River Fort in northwestern Illinois. In other areas of the midwest populated with Yankees from the East, cattle and poultry were more important.[38]

The pork eaten at the site would have come from commercial pork barrels or live herds raised by the settlers. According to Brigham's account books, his store sold both commercial barrels and fresh pork to the miners and other settlers.[39] Pork barrels in which the meat was packed in salt to keep it from rotting were a common way of distributing meat on the frontier in places where butcher shops were rare. According to *Feeding the Frontier Army*, the US Army ran an advertisement for contracts in 1827 specifying that the barrels should "consist of an entire hog to the barrel, except feet, legs, ears, and snout. Should the hog weigh less than 200 pounds, the deficiency must be made of good fat side pieces. One head is allowed to each barrel. The contractor may exclude hams and substitute good side pieces."[40] However, the presence of numerous feet and leg bones at Fort Blue Mounds, as well as parts of the head, suggests that much of the pork during and after the war came from locally raised herds that were allowed to roam free in the countryside.

Pigs or hogs are mentioned in Esau Johnson's memoirs, and he provides the following account of how the animals came to Blue Mounds:

> In the Winter of 1830 I bought a lot of Hogs of Abnor Eads what he drove up to the Leadmines from Illinoise for stock I let them run in the timber there was a heavy crop of Buroak Acorns that season I bought all the Hogs that he had when I saw him which was one hundred and sixteen head And fed them Salt very week and that caused them to stay about holme till spring of 1831 Then they separated about the one half of them went North into the Timber towards the Wisconsin River and the others went into the Timber South of the Blue Mounds on the headwaters of the Pickatonica yet they would come holme once in eight or ten days all summer and fall.[41]

Although details of the account should be read with a grain of salt, the essence of the story is probably factual.

Johnson inserts himself prominently in the account, as he does in other stories in his memoirs, but he and his partner certainly would have had an interest in providing food to their employees. However, I suspect Ebenezer Brigham had a hand in the purchase of the herd since he was the merchant of the community and sold fresh pork from his store. There was indeed a prominent settler named Abner Eads living in Peoria County in northern Illinois at the time, who later served as captain in the Illinois militia during the Black Hawk War. Eads played a major role in the debacle early in the conflict known as Stillman's Run, during which militia attacked Black Hawk's men while they were carrying a white flag signaling Black Hawk's desire to negotiate.[42] Considering his unusual last name, this fellow could be the same pig herder mentioned by Johnson.

While pigs were present at the time of the war, the plea for provisions during the summer of 1832 means that the fort occupants had exhausted their supply of fresh meat obtained by butchering whatever animals they could easily round up. If the fort's request for food was ever honored, meat would have likely come to them in barrels.

Butchered bones from at least four deer show that the settlers adapted to the environment, incorporating wild resources into their diet. Deerskin also provided men of the area with clothing and footwear in the form of moccasins. The oak savannas of southern Wisconsin supported large deer herds, and still do; deer hunting for recreation and meat remains an important part of Wisconsin life. Curiously, excavations at the Apple River Fort produced no deer remains despite the fact it is also situated in good deer country.[43] The only wild animal remains there are from squirrels, ducks, and fish. The lack of deer is probably due to the fort's proximity to the comparatively large population of the thriving town of Galena, the settlers of which would have quickly hunted out large game in the area.

Artifacts and Archaeology of Fort Blue Mounds: A Summary

The large assemblage of artifacts trace the history of Fort Blue Mounds from its beginning as a Black Hawk War fortification though reuse of the fort buildings by miners to its abandonment around 1850, when lead mining ceased to be a major industry in the area. Lead itself was a common find since the settlers made their own ammunition for the few guns they had during the war. Shot, musket balls, and gunflints reflect the defensive purpose of the original structure. Although some unique personal items were unearthed, other aspects of the material culture that we discovered were common and typical of the times. The imported English ceramics, for example, show no great differences in terms of style and type when compared to other settlements of the region with similar socioeconomic status, despite the community's remote location. This is due to the remarkable accessibility of foreign goods and the emphasis put on the social and psychological need to maintain a connection to the "civilized" world. Other material, such as the food remains, however, distinguishes the settlers of Blue Mounds as a frontier people who raised crops and animals and bought food but also subsisted on wild game.

Bits and pieces of the fort, along with the features discovered during the excavations, allow us to reconstruct what the fort looked like: a small, military-style log enclosure with corner blockhouses that were refurbished for later civilian use, with the probable finishing of the interior walls and the addition of glass windows. Artifacts and historical accounts help fill the structure with people. We now know who the people of Fort Blue Mounds were and the dramatic events that took place at the fort during a monumental conflict on the frontier—a conflict that sent the entire population of the region fleeing for cover and ultimately led to a horrific massacre of Indian people. While the Black Hawk War seems almost incomprehensible to us now, stories like that of Fort Blue Mounds allow us to better understand the era. The archaeological artifacts and evidence unearthed during our project enable us to physically connect to the story of this pivotal, tragic, and riveting period in Wisconsin and national history.

❧ Epilogue ❧

As a result of the archaeological discoveries described in this book, the Fort Blue Mounds site has been listed on the National Register of Historic Places, and the fascinating story of the fort and its people has once again captured public interest. In 1993 the Dane County Historical Society put a larger and publicly accessible explanatory marker along County ID in the modern village of Blue Mounds. More recently, the newly formed Blue Mounds Area Historical Society, with the cooperation of the Wisconsin Historical Society and with funds raised for this purpose, replaced the crumbling cement base of the site's 1921 brass plaque. The organization had the original plaque cleaned and reattached to a large boulder characteristic of the geology of the area and donated by nearby Blue Mound State Park. On May 22, 2010, the Blue Mounds Area Historical Society sponsored a rededication ceremony attended by a large crowd. Reflecting the times, the attire was much more casual than the suits and ties and long dresses worn during the original dedication, but the occasion was no less important. Again dignitaries were on hand to affirm the importance of places like Fort Blue Mounds in history. Among those providing comments were Dane County Executive Kathleen Falk, State Senator Jon Erpenbach, and State Representative Sondy Pope-Roberts.

Dane County historical marker in the village of Blue Mounds

___

The Blue Mounds Area Historical Society and local officials will now be working with the Wisconsin Historical Society and private landowners to provide public access to the site of Fort Blue Mounds as well as interpretative signage. Much other work still has to be done, however. In light of the increasing development of the area, the land around the site needs to be permanently protected as parkland so the natural and historical context of this important site is preserved. Otherwise, housing or commercial development could one day surround the small, protected area of the fort, much diminishing its historic character. Such development, in the form of an industrial park, already is impinging on the large hill upon which the site is located, and other lots are for sale nearby. As this book goes to print, county and local officials are examining options for public acquisition.

Additionally, somewhere in the vicinity of the fort, two volunteer soldiers of the Iowa County regiment, William Aubrey and Emerson Green, were buried, and, at some distance away, Henry Dodge's men buried militia volunteer George Force alongside the main trail through the area. All were killed in 1832 while protecting their families and community. It is possible that later residents moved the remains to formal cemeteries developed later in the nineteenth century, but neither graves nor documents have been found

Officials at the new marker on the Fort Blue Mounds site in 2010. From left, Brian Lichte, vice president of the Blue Mounds Area Historical Society; Cindy Downs, president of the Blue Mounds Area Historical Society; Blue Mounds village president Alan Downs.

A reenactment of the arrival of the released Hall girl captives by the Old Lead Mine Region Historical Society took place during the 2010 rededication of the fort's historical marker.

Courtesy of the Blue Mounds Area Historical Society

as yet that shed light on this. It is also possible that the graves remain in their original places, their locations long forgotten as eyewitnesses died off and were replaced by newcomers with no memory of Fort Blue Mounds and the Black Hawk War. Whatever the case, the graves of these men—who are among the earliest of Wisconsin soldiers killed in action—must be located and appropriately marked to honor their service and to ensure that the graves will not be destroyed as development of the area continues.

Perhaps one day, after additional and no doubt exciting archaeological investigations, Fort Blue Mounds will be physically reconstructed, like the Apple River Fort in Illinois. Such an undertaking would bring to life one Black Hawk War story while providing an opportunity for the public to better understand the consequences of the conflict for Native Americans and the settlers who would take their land, as well as the direct role the fort played in the formation of the state of Wisconsin.

≋ Appendix I ≋
Other Forts, Other Stories

Fort Blue Mounds was one of at least seventy-eight settlers' fortifications thrown up in the spring and summer of 1832, twenty-three of which were located in the lead-mining district of Michigan Territory and Illinois. Despite the mounting tensions and violence that foretold major clashes with Native Americans, as well as the formation of volunteer militia in 1827, frontier authorities and settlers seemed unprepared for the new threat of hostilities. A few fortifications already existed from the 1827 Winnebago Uprising, and people flooded the few federal forts. But most settlers had no place to go for protection and had to rapidly fashion fortifications using materials that could be readily obtained or salvaged.

New militia companies quickly formed, but most, like the Fort Blue Mounds company, were untrained and ill-supplied. After the 1827 violence, the US Army beefed up its troop strength at Fort Armstrong in Illinois and Fort Crawford at Prairie du Chien and built Fort Winnebago at the strategic portage between the Fox and Wisconsin Rivers. Ultimately, though, it found itself without sufficient troops to find the elusive Black Hawk and protect the frontier. Reinforcements were called up but never arrived.[1]

The scale of the panic is quite evident not only in the tone of first-hand accounts, but also in the sheer number of fortifications built despite the

FIGURE A.1

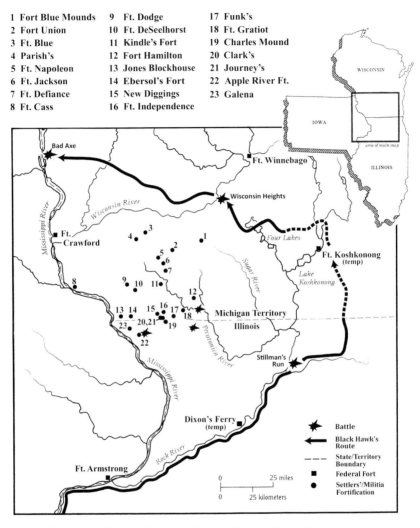

1 **Fort Blue Mounds**	9 **Ft. Dodge**	17 **Funk's**
2 **Fort Union**	10 **Ft. DeSeelhorst**	18 **Ft. Gratiot**
3 **Ft. Blue**	11 **Kindle's Fort**	19 **Charles Mound**
4 **Parish's**	12 **Fort Hamilton**	20 **Clark's**
5 **Ft. Napoleon**	13 **Jones Blockhouse**	21 **Journey's**
6 **Ft. Jackson**	14 **Ebersol's Fort**	22 **Apple River Ft.**
7 **Ft. Defiance**	15 **New Diggings**	23 **Galena**
8 **Ft. Cass**	16 **Ft. Independence**	

Forts of the mining district in Michigan Territory (Wisconsin) and Illinois

Map by Amelia Janes and Robert A. Birmingham

great labor often involved (Figure A.1). Most of these were concentrated in the lead-mining district near Black Hawk's trail in what is now southwestern Wisconsin and northwestern Illinois and in the farming region along in Illinois River, where the settlers feared an uprising by the native population, especially after Potawatomi massacred fifteen people at Indian Creek. Panic spread into neighboring states, and settlers built fortifications in Indiana and even Michigan. Area residents took cover at these fortifications, with the men forming companies of militia to protect their families and neighbors. Other, usually mobile, militia companies formed to patrol areas or to pursue Black Hawk sometimes built separate forts as bases and supply depots.

Like Fort Blue Mounds, the layout of many of the settlers' fortifications followed the frontier military pattern with stout, high wooden stockades and corner log blockhouses that enclosed central buildings. Some communities built structures, also vaguely referred to as "blockhouses" in historical records, that were actually either freestanding buildings or fortified complexes. Many simply built log pickets or stockades around existing buildings including cabins, farm buildings, a school, and a tavern (Figure A.2).

Following an Indian attack in the area that left several dead, miner and merchant George Wallace Jones built a fort at his own personal expense at the large, high geological formation known as Sinsinawa Mound, located near Wisconsin's present-day border with Illinois. Local legend has it that this was the sturdy, two-story stone structure with upper loopholes—narrow gaps used to direct gunfire—that was later converted into a granary when the property was acquired by the illustrious missionary Father Samuel

FIGURE A.2

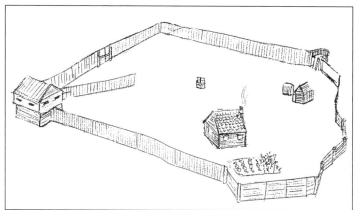

Sketch of Beggs's Fort or Fort Walker in Illinois, based on historical and archaeological information

From *Phase III Data Recovery of Fort Walker (a.k.a. Beggs' Fort II-Wi-1248)*, by M. Catherine Bird and Paula J. Porubcan

Mazzuchelli as a convent for the Catholic Dominican Order. However, Jones himself stated that he built a *log* structure for the protection of his family, slaves, hired hands, and neighbors.[2] (Like Henry Dodge, Jones was a southerner who came to the lead-mining region with black slaves.) After building the fort, Jones left to become aide-de-camp to Colonel Henry Dodge and a militia officer.[3] The stone structure incorporated into the Sinsinawa Dominican Sisters Center was probably built as a storehouse after 1832, possibly by Jones, with the loopholes being an architectural flourish relating to the history of the property and Jones's military service during the Black Hawk War.

Settlers also sought protection at the federal forts built at strategic places throughout the region: Fort Crawford, Fort Dearborn at Chicago, and Fort Winnebago at Portage (Figure A.3). During the pursuit of Black Hawk, the army constructed temporary fortifications for its troops such as the ones at Andalusia in Rock Island County, Illinois, and the log Fort Koshkonong at present-day Fort Atkinson, Wisconsin, a community named for the Black Hawk War fort and the army commander. Fort Koshkonong served as a base of operation for Atkinson and his army during the search for Black Hawk and his band in southern Wisconsin. It is also famously the place where Illinois militia volunteer Abraham Lincoln was mustered out of service.

FIGURE A.3

Federal Fort Winnebago in 1831 at the site of modern-day Portage, Wisconsin

Federal troops also built temporary fortifications at Dixon's Ferry (modern-day Dixon, Illinois) on the Rock River.[4]

As happened at Fort Blue Mounds, people at some of the other settlers' forts suffered death, injuries, and other privations, but most were removed from the conflict and saw no action. Nevertheless, each fort has a unique story that shows the extent the Black Hawk War disrupted life on the frontier during the spring and summer of 1832. Following are some descriptions of notable fortifications in the lead-mining district, and some stories associated with them.

Mineral Point–Area Forts

Mineral Point, named after the mineral lead, had become the center for Michigan Territory lead mining in 1827, shortly after the rich lead deposits had come to the attention of the Americans. Reflecting the comparatively large population, four forts were erected in the vicinity: Fort Union, Fort Jackson, Fort Defiance, and Fort Napoleon (also called Fort Bonaparte). There is little historical information about Fort Napoleon other than that it was located at Diamond Grove lead diggings, three miles northwest of Mineral Point.[5] The others are historically documented although their remnants have not been yet identified.

Fort Union

Fort Union served as the personal headquarters for Henry Dodge, commander of the Iowa County Michigan Territory militia. He simply put a wooden stockade around his homestead and lead furnace, which were located northeast of Mineral Point near present-day Dodgeville. Dodge, one of the most colorful characters in Wisconsin history, moved here in 1827 from Missouri, bringing with him miners, black slaves, and freed slaves employed as workers and servants.[6] As a successful and powerful lead miner, he assumed command of the newly formed Iowa County Michigan Territory militia in 1828 and rode throughout the territory during the Black Hawk War, directing militia activities and engaging Black Hawk's warriors in several bloody battles. It was Dodge and his men who picked up Black Hawk's trail near the Rock River and, along with the Illinois militia, rushed ahead of the regular army, catching up with the band at the Wisconsin River, where the Battle of Wisconsin Heights was fought. Dodge participated in the massacre at Bad Axe on the

Mississippi, and his exploits during the war vaulted him to fame. He went on to serve as the first governor of the Wisconsin Territory, which was formed in 1836 in the wake of rapid Indian removals following the war, and later became a US senator for the state of Wisconsin. A Wisconsin Historical Society historical marker for Fort Union and the Dodge homestead is located on County Y south of Dodgeville.

Fort Jackson

Named for president and former "Indian fighter" Andrew Jackson, Fort Jackson occupied a hill in the center of Mineral Point in the vicinity of the present-day intersection of Commercial and Fountain Streets. It accommodated the residents of the lead-mining community and militia companies formed by area men. Wood was not abundant in this area of prairie and oak openings and was even less available since huge amounts of wood had fueled the furnaces used to melt lead from mined rock. According to George Fiedler, author of *Mineral Point: A History*, "As the preparations for Indian warfare were completed, Mineral Point found itself leveled to the ground except for three buildings. All wood had been used for Fort Jackson."[7]

The fort had blockhouses on the northwest and southeast corners, and a log wall enclosed several cabins for men and their families. The muster roll for the fort lists fifty-eight men who formed a company of the Iowa County Michigan Territory militia.[8] Fort Jackson also served as a base for a company of Dodge's mobile rangers and as the main distribution center for government weapons and supplies to the Michigan Territory militia companies under the charge of US Army Quartermaster George Cole. When the town resumed business after Black Hawk surrendered, residents disassembled the fort, recycling the valuable wood again for buildings and to fuel lead furnaces.

Fort Defiance

Fort Defiance stood on a hill about five miles southeast of Mineral Point on the farm of Daniel M. Parkinson, one of the fort commanders. It reportedly had an 18-foot-high log stockade measuring 80 feet by 120 feet, making it the largest fort in the lead-mining region (Figure A.4).[9] Two blockhouses were located on opposite corners of the fort, and two buildings in the interior housed about forty men, as well as women and children.

FIGURE A.4

Drawing of Fort Defiance by an unknown artist

WHi Image ID 92796

Fort Hamilton

William "Billy" Stephen Hamilton joined other young men who came into the lead region in 1827 to seek their fortune from the mineral.[10] He was the son of Alexander Hamilton, Revolutionary War hero and later secretary of the treasury. Like many of the miners and other settlers, the young Hamilton was a rugged individualist who had rejected the comforts of the East for a more adventurous life.

During the war, Hamilton's miners organized a militia company and built a fort at his diggings at modern-day Wiota, Wisconsin, that looked much like Fort Blue Mounds. It had 40-foot-long log walls, corner blockhouses, and a defensive ditch enclosing a small building (Figure A.5). Given the rank of colonel, Hamilton spent much time away, recruiting Indian allies for the fight against Black Hawk. Like the Blue Mounds and Apple River forts, Fort Hamilton attracted a violent raid by warriors from Black Hawk's band. The events also drew the men of Fort Blue Mounds further into the fray.

On June 14, 1832, a war party from Black Hawk's band attacked and killed five men from the fort as they worked on the nearby farm. Word quickly reached Henry Dodge, who arrived at Fort Hamilton two days later with a group of Ho-Chunk men after stopping at Blue Mounds for fresh horses. Edward Beouchard also left Fort Blue Mounds to support Fort Hamilton with a number of Ho-Chunk men who were on foot.[11] As Dodge arrived at Fort Hamilton, the war party killed another man who had just left the fort, scalping and butchering him "in a most shocking manner."[12] Dodge gathered

FIGURE A.5

William S. Hamilton (inset) and a mural of Fort Hamilton. The mural, painted by John Sargent and Jacob Bissenger on a building in modern-day Wiota, Wisconsin, was based on a 1923 mural by Frank Engebretson.

Inset, WHi Image ID 3458

mounted volunteers from the fort (Hamilton himself was absent at the time), and pursued the war party to a bend in the Pecatonica River, about four miles away, where all eleven Indians were killed in a fierce, close-order clash now commonly called the Battle of Pecatonica or Horseshoe Bend (Figure A.6). Beouchard joined the chase but arrived after the battle. After the clash, Dodge's men took the scalps of the dead warriors and distributed them to Sioux, Menominee, and Ho-Chunk allies gathered at Fort Hamilton. The allied warriors then rushed to the battleground where the dead Indians lay and "cut them literally to pieces."[13] The above instances, once again, illustrate the brutality of war on the frontier.

Apple River Fort

Located at what is now the modern community of Elizabeth in northwestern Illinois, the Apple River Fort was constructed by the lead miners and other residents of the Apple River diggings near Galena. The Apple River Fort was the only fortification of the Black Hawk War to suffer a direct assault by a war

FIGURE A.6

1857 painting of the Pecatonica battleground by Brookes and Stevenson

WHi Image ID 2858

party; in fact, Black Hawk himself led the assault.[14] On June 24, 1832, Black Hawk and approximately two hundred warriors attacked the fort, killing one defender. In his autobiography, Black Hawk said the raid was in reprisal for the militia attack, now known as Stillman's Run, which killed several of his men.[15] At the time, his band was moving north into the Michigan Territory several days' travel away, but the attack on the Apple River Fort was prompted by Black Hawk's dreams and guided by his powerful medicine bags.

Black Hawk left a detailed account of this attack in his autobiography,[16] noting that it began with a dog feast during which he displayed the medicine bags representing the Sauk Nation. These medicine bags were passed down from his ancestors, and he demanded that the warriors protect them. He then set out with the large war party in the direction of the setting sun "following my great medicine bags." On the second night he had a dream that a "great feast" awaited them after one more day of travel. The band then headed for the Apple River settlement, which must have been known to Black Hawk from previous intelligence.

Approaching the fort, the war party happened upon some men who escaped to sound the alarm. Black Hawk and his warriors then attacked the fort, killing one defender in a forty-five-minute exchange of gunfire.[17] Black Hawk retreated, but not before his men took horses and cattle, ransacked houses for food, and set fire to buildings. During the long journey back to camp, the war party encountered militia, which led to another battle. Black Hawk said he lost nine men, including two young chiefs, during this Battle of Kellogg's Grove. The fierce engagement also took the lives of five militia men.

After the war, settlers tore down the Apple River Fort and converted the site to farmland. In 1995 the Apple River Fort Foundation sought to locate

FIGURE A.7

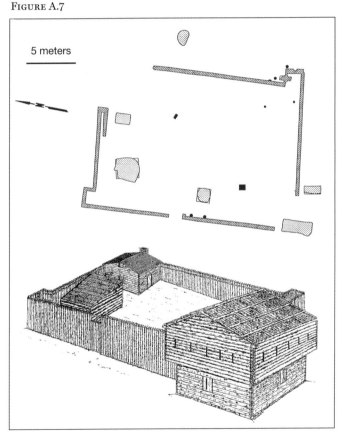

5 meters

Top, archaeological site plan of the Apple River Fort after excavation. Bottom, a drawing of the fort based on historical and archaeological information.

From "'Perfectly Panic Struck': The Archaeology of the Apple River Fort, Jo Daviess County, Illinois"

FIGURE A.8

Reconstructed Apple River Fort at Elizabeth, Illinois

the fort, so it retained the services of Fever River Research headed by archaeologist Floyd Mansberger, who specializes in historic period sites.[18] After
conducting a surface examination of the farm fields, the archaeologists had
the topsoil that had been disturbed by modern plowing removed by heavy
machinery, clearly revealing the remains of walls and other features of the
fort, which were subsequently excavated (Figure A.7). As with Fort Blue
Mounds, the Apple River Fort turned out to be smaller than historical sources
indicated. The archaeological work documented a rectangular structure with
bastions at opposing corners, a blockhouse on a third corner, and a large
cabin that had been incorporated into the fort at the fourth corner.

Thousands of artifacts from the excavations included many of the same
types of objects found at Fort Blue Mounds, and, as with Fort Blue Mounds,
the researchers found that the fort buildings continued to be used for a time
after the war. Based on archaeological and historical documentation, the
Apple River Fort Foundation reconstructed the fort and added an interpretive center. Operated by the Illinois Historic Preservation Agency, it is the
only living history site associated with Black Hawk War (Figure A.8).

⚞ APPENDIX II ⚟
BLACK HAWK WAR SETTLERS' &
MILITIA FORTIFICATIONS

IN 1832 SETTLERS of the Upper Midwest constructed at least seventy-eight fortifications for their protection during the Black Hawk War (Figure A.9). Many of these served as bases for quickly formed companies of militia that would protect settlers and serve as infantry and mounted rangers. Historical documents refer to the fortifications variously as forts, picket stations, palisades, stockades, breastworks, and blockhouses; the term *blockhouse* was used to describe a single building, a one- or two-story cabin-like structure at the corners of a fort, or an entire fort. Some of the sites were simply existing buildings, such as cabins that were fortified for defense.

The following list of Black Hawk War settlers' and militia fortifications was drawn from previous compilations (c.f. Braun, 2000, Jung 2007: 211–213, Wilson and Kaegy 2006, and especially Bird and Porubcan 2001), county and state histories, state archaeological records, published and unpublished articles, and Whitney's (1970–1975) extraordinary three-volume set of Black Hawk War military letters and records. Larry Koschkee of Monroe, Wisconsin, has been researching the locations of Black Hawk War forts for more than a decade and also shared much information for this listing. Many of the sites have not been relocated, and other fortifications may

FIGURE A.9

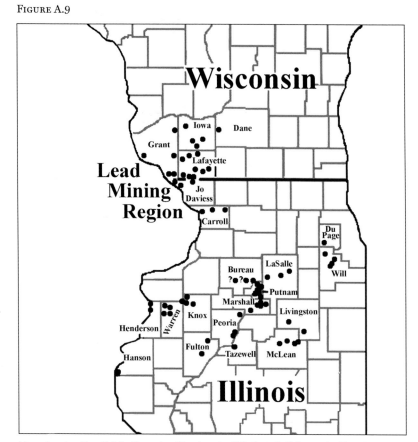

Map showing the distribution of settlers' and militia forts in Wisconsin (then Michigan Territory) and Illinois superimposed on modern counties. Locations are approximate.

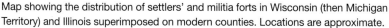

yet be identified through continuing research. Fortifications that were built and used only during the Winnebago Uprising of 1827 are not listed.

Michigan Territory (Wisconsin)

Dane County

Fort Blue Mounds: Rectangular log stockade that covered less than one-quarter acre, with two projecting corner blockhouses and a central log building surrounded by a defensive ditch. It accommodated about fifty settlers; a volunteer company of the Iowa County regiment of the Michigan Territory militia was formed from this group. Three of these men were killed during attacks in the vicinity of the fort.

Grant County

Ebersol's Fort: Sod wall built around the house of Christian Eversoll at Hazel Green. A volunteer militia company was raised by Captain Charles McCoy. (Ref: Holford 1900: 543.)

Fort Cass/Price's Fort: Stockade enclosed log building at Cassville. C. M. Price commanded a company of twenty-eight Michigan Territory militia stationed at the fort. (Refs: Butterfield 1881: 462; Smith 1854: 271–272; Wisconsin Muster Rolls from the Black Hawk War, 1832.)

Fort Dodge or Roundtree's Fort: Circular stockade, 100 feet in diameter, enclosing a two-story blockhouse on the John Roundtree homestead in Platteville. The fortification served as a base for three successive militia companies. The militia muster roll lists thirty-three men under Captain John Oharra. (Refs: Butterfield 1881a: 679; Smith 854: 271–272; Wilgus 1944:68–69; Wisconsin Muster Rolls from the Black Hawk War, 1832.) There was another blockhouse on Blockhouse Creek south of Platteville, which was built and probably only used during the 1827 Winnebago Uprising.

George Jones Blockhouse: Log fortification built on Sinsinawa Mound by George Wallace Jones. It accommodated his family, slaves, hired men, and neighbors. (Refs: Jones 1884: 43–44; Parish 1912: 10, 15.)

Parish's Fort: Fortification built at Wingville (modern Montfort) near the main trail that ran through the lead-mining region, later known as the Military Trail or Road. (Refs: Smith 1854: 271–272; Butterfield 1881a: 861.)

Iowa County

Fort Blue (River): Fortification at the James Jones lead diggings at modern Highland. Jones commanded a Michigan Territory militia company of forty-four men stationed at the fort. (Refs: Butterfield 1881c: 480, 797; Wisconsin Muster Rolls from the Black Hawk War, 1832.)

Fort Jackson: Stockade and two blockhouses located in Mineral Point. The fort protected settlers and operated as a distribution center for military supplies. John Moore's company of fifty-eight Michigan Territory militia was stationed here, and the fort also served as base for James Gentry's mounted company. A historical marker for the fort is located at the intersection of Commerce and Fountain Streets in Dodgeville. (Refs: Crawford and Crawford 1913: 23–24; Smith 1854: 271–272; Wisconsin Muster Rolls from the Black Hawk War, 1832; Whitney 1973: 375.)

Fort Napoleon or Bonaparte: Located on John Terry's property and lead diggings at Diamond Grove, three miles northwest of Mineral Point. Terry commanded a company of fifty-nine Michigan Territory militia at this fort. (Refs: Braun 2000: 9, 10; Smith 1854: 271–272; Wisconsin Muster Rolls from the Black Hawk War, 1832.)

Fort Union: Stockade surrounding the house and headquarters of Michigan Territory militia commander Colonel Henry Dodge near modern Dodgeville, Wisconsin. It also served as a base for a militia company of twenty-six men commanded by Captain Francis Gehon. A Wisconsin Historical Society historical marker for Fort Union and the Dodge homestead is located on County Y south of Dodgeville. (Refs: Smith 1854: 271–272; Wisconsin Muster Rolls from the Black Hawk War, 1832.)

Lafayette County

Fort Defiance: Fort located on the farm of Daniel M. Parkinson, about five miles southeast of Mineral Point, in Willow Springs Township. It consisted of a 120-foot-by-80-foot split-log stockade that had two corner blockhouses enclosing two barracks that accommodated settler families. It was garrisoned by forty volunteers under R. C. Hoard. Parkinson headed a company of mounted militia that fought at Wisconsin Heights and Bad Axe. A historical marker erected in 1995 by the Wisconsin Historical Society is located at the intersection of Highway 23 and Irving Lane. (Refs: Butterfield 1881b: 627; Smith 1854: 271–272; Wisconsin Muster Rolls from the Black Hawk War, 1832.)

Fort DeSeelhorst: A split-log stockade covering one acre and enclosing two blockhouses was located on the farm of Justus DeSeelhorst in Elk Grove Township. Cornelius De Long commanded a company of sixty-seven Michigan Territory militia from this fortification. (Refs: Butterfield 1881b: 602–603; Smith 1854: 271–272; Wisconsin Muster Rolls from the Black Hawk War, 1832.)

Fort Funk or Funk's Fort: This fort in modern Monticello Township was manned by a Michigan Territory militia company of thirty-one men under the command of Benj. Funk. (Refs: Butterfield 1881b: 427; Whitney 1970: 261; Wisconsin Muster Rolls from the Black Hawk War, 1832.)

Fort Gratiot: A stockade and blockhouse at Gratiot's Grove were built during the 1827 Winnebago Uprising and further strengthened during the Black Hawk War. Fifty-six men served as a Michigan Territory militia company under the command of Fortunatus Berry. (Refs: Smith 1854: 271–272; Wisconsin Muster Rolls from the Black Hawk War, 1832.)

Fort Hamilton: This log stockade, 40 feet on a side and enclosing a 16-by-24-foot building on the west, was built by lead miner William "Billy" Stephen

Hamilton, son of Alexander Hamilton, at his diggings near the Pecatonica River at Wiota. It had two corner blockhouses surrounded by a defensive ditch. The fort garrison consisted of fifty-four volunteers. Six settler men were killed by Sauk in the vicinity, leading to the Battle of Pecatonica or Horseshoe Bend. An artist's conception of the fort can be found on a painted mural on the side of a building along Highway 78 in Wiota, along with a historical marker. (Refs: Bisegger et al. 1993; Butterfield 1881b: 609; Smith 1854: 271–272; Wisconsin Muster Rolls from the Black Hawk War, 1832.)

Fort Independence: Stockade built of split logs in a wall trench at the Shullsburg lead diggings, probably near the John Coons cabin. Thirty-one militia volunteers were stationed here under the command of Isaac Hamilton. (Refs: Smith 1854: 271–272; Butterfield 1881: 581–584; Wisconsin Muster Rolls from the Black Hawk War, 1832.)

Kindle's Fort: This fort was located on the farm of James Kindle Sr. in Kendall Township. (Ref: Butterfield 1881b: 624.)

New Diggings: Fort located on the farm of Abraham Looney at New Diggings, just north of the Illinois border. A company of sixty-nine men was raised from area miners and was considered to be a part of the Jo Daviess County Illinois militia. (Refs: Beers and Co. 1901: 360, 743; Whitney 1973: 428; Wisconsin Muster Rolls from the Black Hawk War, 1832.)

White Oaks Forts: Two forts were built in White Oaks Springs Township. The largest was 100 feet by 50 feet and was built by S. M. Journey. Capt. Benj. Clark formed a Michigan Territory mounted militia company of seventy-eight men there. A smaller, unnamed fort, 50 feet square, was built somewhere nearby. (Refs: Butterfield 1881b: 584–585; Whitney 1973: 427; Wisconsin Muster Rolls from the Black Hawk War, 1832.)

Illinois

Bureau County

Fort Thomas: Blockhouse and stockade built at the tavern and stagecoach stop owned by Henry Thomas. (Ref: Whitney 1973: 663.)

Hartzell's Fort: Log blockhouse built on the site of Thomas Hartzell's abandoned store above Hennepin by settlers and John Strawn's Illinois militia company. (Refs: Ellsworth 1880: 79–80; Ford 1860: 54; Whitney 1970: 638–639.)

Joel Doolittle Cabin: Fortified cabin. (Ref: Leonard 1968: 221–222.)

Carroll County

Crane's Fort: Fortified house at Cherry Grove surrounded by a breastwork abatis built by Thomas Crane. (Refs: H. F. Kett and Co. 1878: 271; Whitney 1970: 490.)

Plum River Fort: Blockhouse built on a point near the Mississippi River bluffs at modern Savanna and occupied for a short time by men of the community before they joined their families at Galena. (Ref: Whitney 1970: 291, 421–423.)

DuPage County

Fort Payne: Stockade, 100 feet square, with two corner blockhouses, located on the DuPage River at modern-day Naperville. It was built and garrisoned by Illinois militia volunteers from Danville. A reconstruction of the fort is located at the Naper Settlement Museum complex on South Webster Street and operated by the Naperville Heritage Society. A historical marker is located on Highway 34 in Naperville. (Refs: Whitney 1973: 597–99; Whitney 1975: 1001; Blanchard 1882: 42–43.)

Fulton County

Fort Holcomb: Breastwork in Putnam Township. (Ref: Chapman 1879: 302–303.)

Wright's Fort: Blockhouse and stockade in Canton Township. (Ref: Chapman 1879: 295.)

Hancock County

Spillman's Fort: Blockhouse and stockade on the property of Hezekan Spillman. (Ref: Gregg 1880: 509.)

Henderson County

Fort Pence: Fortification built by John Pence north of modern-day Oquawka on the Mississippi River. (Refs: Lake City Publishing Co. 1894: 414; Whitney 1973: 199.)

Yellow Banks: Fort built as a base for a company of mounted Illinois militia at Oquawka. (Refs: Whitney 1970: 457; 1975: 662–663.)

Jo Daviess County

Apple River Fort: Rectangular log stockade with bastions at opposing corners, a blockhouse on a third corner, and a large cabin incorporated into the fort at the fourth corner. Black Hawk and a large force attacked the fort, leading to the deaths of one fort defender and several Sauk. The fort site in Elizabeth was completely excavated by archaeologists in 1995. A reconstruction was built based on historical and archaeological information and is operated as an Illinois state historic site. (Ref: Mansberger and Stratton 1996.)

Fort Charles or Scales Fort: Samuel Scales commanded a company of Illinois militia volunteers at this fortification located in Council Hill Township on the

Charles Mound near the Apple River, fourteen miles from the Apple River Fort. (Refs: Whitney 1970: 519–520; Whitney 1975: 723.)

Galena Blockhouse or Stockade Refuge: Large log stockade with two blockhouses and several fortified houses in the lead-mining community of Galena, which also served as a major depot for federal military supplies distributed to militia. (Refs: Carter 1959; Whitney 1973: 421–423.)

Knox County

Fort Aggie: This fort was located on the Rio Township property of John Cresswell and named for his wife. (Ref: Chapman and Co. 1878: 485.)

Fort Lewis: Timber stockade, 210 feet square, in Henderson Township, with loopholes and two corner clapboard-covered blockhouses, enclosing a shed. (Ref: Chapman and Co. 1878: 152–153.)

Gum's Fort: Fortification built around the cabin of John Gum at Henderson's Grove. It accommodated twenty-five families and served as a base for an infantry company of the Illinois militia. (Refs: Whitney 1973: 73, 170; Whitney 1975: 662.)

McMurtry's Fort: Stockade and blockhouse on the William McMurtry farmstead on Middle Creek, three miles northwest of Henderson's Grove in Sparta Township. A company of Illinois-mounted militia was stationed at the fort. (Ref: Chapman and Co. 1878: 152.)

LaSalle County

Fort Johnson or Fort Ottawa: Blockhouse and stockade located on the south bank of the Illinois River, opposite the mouth of the Fox River in South Ottawa. Builder James Johnson commanded a regiment of volunteer Illinois militia from this fortification. A historical marker is located in Ottawa at the junction of Highways 71 and 23. (Refs: Hoffman 1906: 56; Rasmusen 1992: 193; Whitney 1973: 418.)

Fort Wilbourn (also referred to as Deposit and Horn): Stockade and storehouse built on a bluff on the Illinois River, south of LaSalle, and occupied by two companies of Illinois militia under the command of Reddick Horn. A historical marker is located at the intersection of Orlando Smith Road and Highway 351. (Refs: Whitney 1970: 479; Whitney 1973: 406, 417; Whitney 1975: 1227.)

Green's Fort: The fortified cabin of James Green on Shoal Creek, eight miles southwest of Greenville. (Ref: Hoffman 1906: 69.)

Livingston County

Unnamed blockhouse at Little Vermilion Settlement. (Ref: Hasbrouck 1924: 147–148.)

Marshall County

Beckwith's Fort: Picket around cabin in Roberts Township. (Ref: Ellsworth 1880: 413.)

Dever's Fort: A log stockade measuring 100 feet by 80 feet, with two opposing blockhouses, enclosing the cabin of James Dever at Round Prairie. Settlers lived in tents within the stockade. (Refs: Ellsworth 1880: 125; Forde 1860: 49.)

Fort Darnell: Split-log stockade surrounding new cabins on the Benjamin Darnell farm along Sandy Creek in Evans Township. (Refs: Ford 1860: 49; Ellsworth 1880: 125, 440–441.)

Griffith's Fort: Stockade of split logs with loopholes in Roberts Township. (Refs: Ellsworth 1880: 413; Whitney 1973: 748.)

Roberts's Fort: Picket around Jesse Roberts's cabin two miles south of Magnolia, which accommodated seven or eight families. (Refs: Ellsworth 1880: 125, 407–408, 413; Forde 1860: 49; Whitney 1973: 748, 1339.)

McLean County

Bartholomew's Fort: Blockhouse in Money Creek Township. (Ref: Hasbrouck 1924: 147–148.)

Fort Henline: Log stockade with opposing blockhouses on the John Henline farm in Lawndale Township, enclosing about half an acre of split logs in a trench along Henline Creek. (Ref: Watson 1976.)

Mackinaw Timber Fort: Fortification built by Captain Merritt Covell's company of Illinois militia near present-day Lawndale. (Ref: Whitney 1970: 565.)

Patton's Fort: Fortified farmhouse of James Patton near Lexington. The property is now owned by the McLean County Historical Society. (Refs: Hasbrouck 1924: 102, 107, 147–148.)

Peoria County

Bureau Grove: Illinois militia fortification commanded by Major Samuel Bogart. (Refs: Whitney 1973: 662–663.)

Fort Clark: Located on the Illinois River in modern Peoria. (Ref: Slane 1933: 27–30.)

Fort Defiance or Reed's Fort: Fort in Hallock Township, LaSalle Prairie, manned by volunteer Illinois militia commanded by John Gay. (Refs: Whitney 1973: 542, 555–556.)

Putnam County

Boyle's Fort: Located in Magnolia Township. (Refs: Ellsworth 1880: 15, 248; Ford 1860: 50.)

Fort Cribs or Willis' Fort: Stockade surrounding a large barn and corncribs belonging to James Willis, near modern Florid. The enclosure accommodated twenty-two families and served as a base for Illinois militia mounted rangers. (Refs: Ford 1860: 50; Whitney 1975: 747–748.)

Fort Hennepin: Fortified traders' cabin in Hennepin. (Refs: Ford 1860: 50; Whitney 1970: 638–639.)

Fort Warnock: On John Warnock's farm near Granville. (Refs: Ellsworth 1880: 124; Ford 1860: 50; Whitney 1975: 748.)

Hannum or Horram's Fort: Stockade with opposing bastions in Magnolia Township. (Refs: Ford 1860: 50; Whitney 1973: 748.)

Leeper's Fort: Picketed house of John Leeper in Granville Township. (Refs: Ellsworth 1880: 125; Ford 1860: 50; Whitney 1975: 747–748.)

Strawn's Fort: Stockaded cabin in Magnolia Township. (Refs: Ellsworth 1880: 217; Whitney 1975: 747–748.)

Tazewell County

"Fort Dolittle": It is so nicknamed because of the lack of action there. (Refs: Howard 1972: 150; Whitney 1973: 424.)

Warren County

Buffin's Fort: Stockade and blockhouse at modern-day Denny in Sumner Township. (Refs: H. F. Kett and Co. 1877: 167; Whitney 1975: 1258, 1260.)

Butler's Fort: Stockade and blockhouse in Monmouth Township at the home of Peter Butler that accommodated about twenty families. It also served as the base for a mounted Illinois militia unit. (Ref: Bateman and Selby 1903: 953.)

Findley's Blockhouse: Located in Hale Township. (Ref: Whitney 1975: 1258, 1260.)

Martin's Blockhouse: Located in Sumner Township. (Refs: Whitney 1975: 986, 1258, 1260.)

Will County

Fort Des Plaines or Nonsense: Stockade and blockhouse on the Des Plaines River at modern Joliet. (Refs: Maue 1928: 266; Woodruff 1878: 374; Whitney 1973: 518–519, 597–599.)

Fort Walker or Beggs's Fort: Wooden enclosure around the farm buildings of Rev. Beggs, used for protection by the people of Plainfield until they left for Fort Dearborn at Chicago. It also served as a base for mounted militia patrolling the area. Archaeologists have completely excavated the complex, locating the remnants of the enclosure and buildings associated with the farmstead. (Refs: Beggs 1868: 99, 253–255; Bird and Porubcan 2001.)

McKee's Fort: Fortified house. (Ref: Woodruff 1878: 281.)

Orr's Blockhouse: Honey Creek supply depot for Illinois militia. (Ref: Whitney 1975: 777, 1001, 1346–1347.)

Sisson's Fort: Located on the Des Plaines River at Lockport. (Refs: Stevens 1907: 91; Maune 1928: 229; Woodruff 1874: 21.)

Indiana and Michigan

Although far from Black Hawk's actual movements, Indiana and Michigan were not free from panic, leading to the activation of the Indiana militia (Loftus 2003) and the building of several settlers' fortifications in Indiana and one in Michigan. The settler's feared not only Black Hawk but also uprisings of local Potawatomi. In two cases, the fortifications were never completed after initial alarms. Fort Beane in Goshen, Indiana, was one of these (Charles C. Chapman and Co. 1881: 440); a historical marker on a boulder at the intersection of Reynolds Street and Highway 33 in Goshen commemorates the event. Other fortifications built for the protection of settlers in Indiana were at least started in the communities of South Bend and Brighton (then Lexington), at Door Prairie in LaPorte County, and on an island in Cedar Lake in Lake County (Andreas 1884: 118–119; Goodspeed 1882: 224–225; Stanfield 1880: 449–453). In Michigan, settlers of St. Joseph County began building Fort Hogan on the Hogan farm in August 1832 because of rumors of an imminent attack by Potawatomi from a small neighboring settlement. Work halted after it was determined that the rumors were unfounded (Halsey 1991: 10; Pioneer Society of the State of Michigan 1880: 489–500).

Appendix III
Features & Associated Artifacts
Found Below the Modern Plow Zone
at Fort Blue Mounds

No. 1

Location: S25 E0

Description: Dark circular stain 4 in. in diameter

Interpretation: Possible small post mold

No. 2

Location: S10 E20; S15 E15; S20 E10; S25 E0, E5; S35 W10; S40 W10, W15; S5 W40; S10 W40

Description: Dark linear feature oriented NE/SW that narrowed with depth to 1-ft. wide trench that was 2-ft. deep, as measured from the top of the present land surface to the bottom of the feature. Feature becomes shallow and terminates where it meets shallow bedrock in the area of the eastern blockhouse. Forty ft. SW of this point, it turns 90 degrees to NW and continues 42 ft., where it terminates at the area of the western blockhouse. Contained remains of wooden post and several circular widenings represent locations of former large posts.

Artifacts: metal button, shell button, clay pipe fragment, 1 percussion cap, 5 pieces lead sprue, 24 melted pieces of lead waste, part to broken shovel or pick, 2 shards bottle glass, 7 ceramic sherds (blue transferprint [TFP], undecorated, unidentified), 7 pieces animal bone (pig, deer, unidentified), 17 machine-cut (MC) nails, 2 handwrought (HW) nails, small pieces of window glass, small pieces of brick and/or daub/chinking.

Interpretation: 1832 fort stockade trench

No. 2a

Location: S15 E20

Description: Wide, shallow, dark feature 5 ft. to the NW of Feature 2 stockade trench. Contained small rocks, charcoal, ash.

Interpretation: 1832 SE defensive ditch

No. 2b, c

Location: S25 E0, E5

Description: Circular widenings in stockade trench, Feature 2.

Artifact: 1 unidentified ceramic sherd.

Interpretation: Locations of former stockade posts

No. 3, 4

Location: N20 W5

Description: Shallow, linear stains oriented E/W at base of plow zone

Interpretation: Furrows from modern plowing

No. 5

Location: S40 E0

Description: Top of filled-in defensive ditch covering much of unit. Only top 24 in. were archaeologically excavated to get plan.

Artifacts: 1 white clay pipe bowl, 2 bottle glass shards, 9 ceramic sherds (plain, blue TFP), percussion cap, lead sprue, 5 pieces melted lead waste, 4 unidentified animal remains.

Interpretation: Defensive ditch, same as Features 2a, 6

No. 6

Location: S40 W10; S45 W15

Description: Dark trench with many rocks in SE part of unit running parallel to stockade trench. Top 16 in. archaeologically excavated in S40 W10 but taken down to the top of bedrock in S45 W15, where feature was nearly 4 ft. deep.

Artifacts: base to wine bottle, 9 plain ceramic sherds, part of metal pail or bucket, 1 gunflint, 1 shot, 2 fragments lead sprue, 7 melted lead waste pieces, 1 modern lead bullet, 31 animal remains (pig, unidentified mammal), tin can fragments, 1 MC nail, 1 unidentified nail, small pieces window glass.

Interpretation: Filled-in defensive ditch same as Features 2a, 5

No. 7

Location: S10 E10

Description: Large, irregular pit measuring 6 ft. x 5 ft. in extent and 20 in. deep and filled with ash, charcoal, and burned and unburned debris. Top is truncated by plow zone. Original pit may have been oval or square.

Artifacts: 1 bone button, 1 clay pipe fragment, 33 burned and unburned ceramic sherds (blue TFP, red TFP, plain, brown TFP Texian Campaigne pattern dish, hand-painted sprig, plain, 1 shot, 89 small burned and unburned animal remains (pig, deer, unidentified mammal), 5 MC nails and 3 fragments, 1 HW nail, 1 unidentified nail, small brick fragments, window glass.

Interpretation: Ash/trash pit next to blockhouse/later cabin, dating to circa 1840s

No. 8

Location: S10 E25

Description: Partially excavated, round-bottomed pit or depression at north side of unit and extending into unexcavated area. It is 17 in. wide, 45 in. long, and extends to top of bedrock at a depth of 1 ft. below modern surface of ground. No artifacts.

Interpretation: Possible shallow storage or cache pit for blockhouse/later cabin

No. 9

Location: S15 E20

Description: Small layer of ash and charcoal 2 in. thick at base of plow zone.

Artifacts: 4 bottle glass shards (including scroll-style whiskey flask), 1 unprocessed lead (galena) piece, 1 piece melted lead waste.

Interpretation: Top of defensive ditch fill

No. 10, 11

Location: S15 E20

Description: Small, thin ash layers at base of plow zone

Interpretation: Deposit associated with Feature 7

No. 12

Location: S35 W10

Description: One-ft.-wide trench (stockade) excavated to 16 in. below modern surface of ground.

Artifacts: 3 unidentified ceramic sherds.

Interpretation: Stockade trench same as Feature 2

No. 13

Location: S5 W15

Description: Ash, charcoal, daub or disintegrating brick concentration 12 in. x 18 in. in extent and 15 in. deep from present surface. Disturbed by modern plowing. Much melted lead found in vicinity.

Interpretation: Lead processing area

No. 14

Location: N10 W15

Description: Circular pile of weathered, unmodified chert stones or cobbles 33 in. diameter. Chert cobbles are similar to those found throughout soils of the site area.

Interpretation: Either an unusual natural formation of weathered chert or the result of human activity such as clearing rocks from the dirt floor of a structure

No. 15

Location: N10 W15

Description: Ash, charcoal, and daub or brick fragments below plow zone in west wall of unit that is 16 in. wide, 18 in. long, and 15 in. deep, as measured from surface of the ground. Top disturbed by modern plowing.

Artifacts: Melted lead pieces.

Interpretation: Lead processing area

No. 16

Location: S10 W40; S15 W35, W40; S20 W30, W35, W40; S25 W25, W30, W35; S30 W20, W25, W30; S35 W20, W25, W30, W35; S40 W20, W25

Description: Wide ditch along SW wall of fort running parallel to stockade trench and filled with dirt, ash, charcoal, rocks, and artifacts, many of which had burned. It measures 45 ft. long from the south corner of the fort to the west end, where it abutted the western blockhouse. It ranges 4 ft. to 7 ft. in width and it was originally dug to the top of bedrock or about 3 ft. deep at center. The top 1 ft. to 2 ft. was archaeologically excavated to define the limits, leaving the bottom of feature intact for future investigation.

Artifacts: 2 fragments clay pipe, 1 pin, 1 thimble, 1 burned gunflint/fire starter, 2 shot, 1 percussion cap, 1 unprocessed lead (galena) piece, 5 pieces lead waste, 4 bottle glass shards, 55 burned and unburned ceramic sherds (plain, yellowware, glazed redware, hand-painted floral, blue edge decorated, TFP blue, TFP blue Villa in the Regent's Park, London pattern dish), 67 burned and unburned animal remains (pig, deer, cow, unidentified bird), 6 MC nails and 10 fragments, 2 HW nails, 6 unidentified nail fragments, 1 horseshoe nail, brick fragments, daub, window glass.

Interpretation: SW defensive ditch later filled in with debris, ash, and rock. Much of the debris is burned.

No. 17

Location: N10 E0

Description: Short, linear, sandy disturbance

Interpretation: Rodent burrow

No. 18

Location: N0 W45; N5 W40, W45; N15 W30; N25 W15

Description: Trench 4 to 5 ft. wide and 3 ft. deep that appears to abut area of western blockhouse and continues along NW side of fort. Large rock and stone concentration and high density of artifacts at SW end adjacent to western blockhouse/later cabin area.

Artifacts: bone button, 3 glass beads, 10 fragments white clay pipes, fragments from clay elbow-style pipe, 1 bale seal part, 1 bottle glass shard, 6 shot, 1 gunflint, 1 lead sprue, 11 unprocessed lead (galena) pieces, 86 ceramic sherds (blue TFP, green edge decorated, blue edge decorated, hand-painted broad floral and sprig, annular, undecorated), 187 animal remains (pig, deer, chicken, grouse, fish, unidentified mammal and bird), 2 HW nails, 19 MC nails, 8 unidentified nails and 3 fragments, brass tack, window glass, daub or chinking (some whitewashed), 5 pieces slag.

Interpretation: NW defensive ditch

No. 19

Location: N5 W45

Description: E/W oriented shallow, linear disturbance on Feature 18.

Artifacts: 15 ceramic sherds (TFP blue, blue edge decorated, porcelain, unidentified burned), 26 animal remains (pig, deer, unidentified mammal and bird), 1 modern wire nail, 3 MC nails, 4 unidentified nail fragments.

Interpretation: Modern plow scar

No. 20

Location: S5 E0

Description: Partially excavated disintegrating brick platform 35 in. x 45 in.

extent and 2½ in. thick, truncated by plow zone at depth of 8 in. It extends N and W into unexcavated areas.

Interpretation: Fireplace or forge platform, probably a part of central building of fort

No. 21

Location: N5 W50

Description: Large circular disturbance with bottom of cement post

Interpretation: 1921 cement marker

No. 22

Location: N5 W45

Description: Ash layer in upper part of Feature 18

Interpretation: Defensive ditch fill

No. 23

Location: N0 W40

Description: Deep, dark soil disturbance in NW corner of unit.

Artifacts: US military button, 1837 silver coin, 2 unprocessed lead (galena) pieces, 49 plain ceramic sherds, 4 animal remains (unidentified mammal), 1 HW nail, 1 unidentified nail fragment, window glass.

Interpretation: Side of SW defensive ditch, same as Feature 18. Filled after 1838.

No. 24

Location: N25 W0, W5

Description: Dark linear trench, 1 ft. wide and 2 ft. deep, oriented NE/SW and turns 90 degrees to the SE.

Interpretation: Stockade trench and north corner of fort

No. 25

Location: N35 E5

Description: Large, deep feature of dark soil with a thick lens or layer of lighter soil within it. The feature extends down 2½ ft. to bedrock, as measured from present land surface. The bottom of a 1921 cement marker post was found next to feature.

Artifacts: 4 fragments dark-green wine bottle shards, 2 animal remains (pig tooth, unidentified mammal).

Interpretation: North corner of defensive ditch

 NOTES

Chapter 1

1. John Reynolds to the Militia of the Northwestern Section of the State, April 16 (?) 1832, in *The Black Hawk War, 1831–1832*, comp. and ed. Ellen M. Whitney, vol. 2, part 1 (Springfield: Illinois State Historical Library, 1973), 264–265.

2. Henry Dodge to Henry Atkinson, May 16, 1832, in Whitney, *Black Hawk War*, vol. 2, part 1, 375.

3. Alice E. Smith, *The History of Wisconsin: From Exploration to Statehood*, vol. 1 (Madison: State Historical Society of Wisconsin, 1973), 130. Patrick J. Jung, *The Black Hawk War of 1832* (Norman: University of Oklahoma Press, 2007), 103.

4. Jung, *The Black Hawk War of 1832*, 172.

5. Kent Nerburn, *Chief Joseph & the Flight of the Nez Perce: The Untold Story of an American Tragedy* (New York: Harper Collins, 2006).

6. See for example Roger L. Nichols, "The Black War in Retrospect," *Wisconsin Magazine of History* 65, no. 4 (Summer 1982): 239–246; Roger L. Nichols, *Black Hawk and the Warrior's Path* (Arlington Heights, IL: Harlan Davidson, 1992); Patrick J. Jung, "The Black Hawk War Reconsidered: A New Interpretation of its Causes and Consequences," *Journal of the Indian Wars* 1, no. 2 (1999): 30–69; Anthony F. C. Wallace, "Prelude to Disaster: The Course of Indian-White Relations Which Led to the Black Hawk War of 1832," in *The Black Hawk War, 1831–1832*, comp. and ed. Ellen M. Whitney, vol. 1, part 1 (Springfield: Illinois State Historical Library, 1970), 1–51.

7. John B. Patterson, ed., *Life of Ma-ka-tai-me-she-kia-kiak or Black Hawk* (St. Louis, 1882), 138.

8. Donald Jackson, ed., *Black Hawk: An Autobiography* (Urbana: University of Illinois Press, 1964); *The Black Hawk War, 1831–1832*, comp. and ed. Ellen M. Whitney, 3 volumes (Springfield: Illinois State Historical Library, 1970–1975). Detailed modern historical accounts of the Black Hawk War are: Kerry A. Trask, *Black Hawk: The Battle for the Heart of America* (New York: Henry Holt and Company, 2007) and Jung, *The Black Hawk War of 1832*. As noted by Donald Jackson in the preface of *Black Hawk: An Autobiography*, a caveat in the use of the autobiography is that Black Hawk dictated it through an interpreter, Antoine LeClaire, and this was edited by newspaper editor John P. Patterson. Although modern scholars believe the work is authentic, there is no way to know if all words attributed to Black Hawk are completely his. Patterson made changes in wording and added new material in a later edition, still attributing the words to Black Hawk.

9. Nichols, *Black Hawk and the Warrior's Path*, 113.

10. Jackson, *Black Hawk: An Autobiography*, 49, 139; Nichols, *Black Hawk and the Warrior's Path*, 17.

11. Jackson, *Black Hawk: An Autobiography*, 110.

12. Benjamin Drake, *Life of Tecumseh and of His Brother the Prophet; With a Historical Sketch of the Shawanoe Indians* (Mount Vernon: Rose Press, 2008); Alice Beck Kehoe, *The Ghost Dance: Ethnohistory and Revitalization*, 2nd ed. (Long Grove, IL: Waveland Press, 2006).

13. Jackson, *Black Hawk: An Autobiography*, 116.

14. Jung, *The Black Hawk War of 1832*, 73.

15. Jackson, *Black Hawk: An Autobiography*, 139.

16. Ibid., 120.

17. John W. Hall, *Uncommon Defense: Indian Allies in the Black Hawk War* (Cambridge, MA: Harvard University Press, 2009).

18. Jackson, *Black Hawk: An Autobiography*, 120.

19. Daniel Parkinson, "Pioneer Life in Wisconsin," in *Collections of the State Historical Society of Wisconsin*, ed. Lyman Copeland Draper, vol. 2 (Madison: State Historical Society of Wisconsin, 1856), 356.

20. Jonathan Carver, *Travels through the Interior Parts of North America, in the Years 1766, 1767, and 1768* (Minneapolis: Ross and Haines, 1965), 46–47.

21. An archaeological survey of part of the Wisconsin Heights battlefield funded by the Wisconsin Historical Society yielded two musket balls. One was found on a slope occupied by militia during the battle and apparently fired at them.

Examination by the author suggests that it once was a small lead decorative brooch melted into a musket ball.

22. Jackson, *Black Hawk: An Autobiography*, 139.

Chapter 2

1. Zachary Taylor to Henry Atkinson, June 1, 1832, in *The Black Hawk War, 1831–1832*, comp. and ed. Ellen M. Whitney, vol. 2, part 1, 499–500.

2. Charles C. Chapman, *History of Fulton County, Illinois* (Peoria: Charles C. Chapman and Co., 1879), 302.

3. H. A. Tenney, "Early Times in Wisconsin," in *First Annual Report and Collections of the State Historical Society of Wisconsin*, vol. 1 (Madison: State Historical Society of Wisconsin, 1855), 94–95.

4. "Beouchard's Narrative," in *The History of Wisconsin in Three Parts, Historical, Documentary, and Descriptive*, ed. William Smith, part 2 (Madison: B. Brown, 1854), 209; "John Messersmith's Narrative," in *The History of Wisconsin in Three Parts*, ed. William Smith, part 2 (Madison: B. Brown, 1854), 225.

5. "Messersmith's Narrative, in *The History of Wisconsin in Three Parts*, part 2, 224–226; "Beouchard's Narrative," in *The History of Wisconsin in Three Parts*, 209; "Edward D. Beouchard's Vindication," in *Report and Collections of the State Historical Society of Wisconsin*, vol. 7 (Madison: State Historical Society of Wisconsin, 1876), 289–296; Esau Johnson Papers, 1800–1882, Wisconsin Historical Society Archives; Ebenezer Brigham Papers, 1816–1887, Wisconsin Historical Society Archives.

6. Whitney, *Black Hawk War*, vol. 2, parts 1 and 2.

7. "Beouchard's Narrative," in *The History of Wisconsin in Three Parts*, 209; Esau Johnson Papers.

8. Muster Roll of Captain Sherman's Company of Iowa Militia Stationed at Blue Mounds Fort, Wisconsin Historical Society, from Wisconsin Muster Rolls from the Black Hawk War, 1832, typescript of the original muster rolls in the records of the General Accounting Office (Record Group 217) at the National Archives, Washington, DC, www.wisconsinhistory.org/turningpoints/search.asp?id=1586; "Beouchard's Narrative" in *The History of Wisconsin in Three Parts*, 209; Esau Johnson Papers.

9. John Sherman, Blue Mounds Fort, to Henry Dodge, May 30, 1832, in Whitney, *Black Hawk War*, vol. 2, part 1, 487.

10. S. R. Beggs, *Pages from the Early History of the West and North-West* (Cincinnati: R. P. Thompson, 1868), 90; *History of Fulton County, Illinois*, 302.

11. *The History of Jo Daviess County, Chicago, Illinois* (Chicago: H. F. Kett and Co., 1878), 292.

12. A partial letter to Henry Dodge dated June 4, 1832, in the Ebenezer Brigham Papers, probably written by Brigham, reads: "Sir Having learned there had arrived at Galena some small cannon & swivels I have taken the liberty to ask your aid in getting one of them. The bearer Mr. Collins will proceed to Galena and should this request be granted return with all speed . . ."

13. Esau Johnson Papers.

14. George M. Crawford and Robert Crawford, eds., *Memoirs of Iowa County: From the Earliest Historical Times Down to the Present* (Chicago: Northwestern Historical Association, 1913), 25.

15. Ebenezer Brigham Papers.

16. Esau Johnson Papers.

17. Four Lakes Council, in Whitney, *Black Hawk War*, vol. 2, part 1, 454–456; Blue Mounds Council, May 28, 1832, in Whitney, *Black Hawk War*, vol. 2, part 1, 467–469.

18. Anthony F. C. Wallace, "Prelude to Disaster," 1–51.

19. Henry Atkinson to Henry Gratiot, May 27, 1832, in Whitney, *Black Hawk War*, vol. 2, part 2, 1973, 457–458.

20. John Sherman to Henry Dodge, May 30, 1832, in Whitney, *Black Hawk War*, vol. 2, part 1, 487–488.

21. Richard C. Taylor, "Notes Respecting Certain Indian Mounds and Earthworks in the Form of Animal Effigies, Chiefly in Wisconsin Territory, U.S.," *American Journal of Science and Art* 34 (1838): 88–104.

22. Esau Johnson Papers.

23. Porter's Grove Council, June 3–4, 1832, in Whitney, *Black Hawk War*, vol. 2, part 1, 507–513; Henry Gratiot to Henry Atkinson, June 6, 1832, in Whitney, *Black Hawk War*, vol. 2, part 1, 1973, 531–532; Henry Gratiot to William Clark, June 12, 1832, in Whitney, *Black Hawk War*, vol. 2, part 1, 577–579; Henry Gratiot Diary, in Whitney, *Black Hawk War*, vol. 2, part 2, 1303.

24. Esau Johnson Papers.

25. James M. Stode to Henry Atkinson, June 10, 1832, in Whitney, *Black Hawk War*, vol. 2, part 1, 566–569.

26. Council with the Rock River Winnebago, September 11, 1832, in Whitney, *Black Hawk War*, vol. 2, part 2, 1133.

27. Henry Dodge, Fort Union to Henry Atkinson, June 18, 1832, in Whitney, *Black Hawk War*, vol. 1, part 2, 622–625.

28. "Beouchard's Narrative," in *The History of Wisconsin in Three Parts*, 209.

29. Ibid.

30. Ebenezer Brigham Papers.

31. Henry Dodge to Henry Atkinson, June 30, 1832, in Whitney, *Black Hawk War*, vol. 2, part 2, 715; Parkinson, "Pioneer Life in Wisconsin," 351.

32. Henry Atkinson to Roger Jones, in Whitney, *Black Hawk War*, vol. 2, part 2, 1210.

33. Esau Johnson Papers.

34. Meriwether L. Clark to William Clark, July 25, 1832, in Whitney, *Black Hawk War*, vol. 2, part 2, 877–878.

35. Esau Johnson Papers.

36. "Beouchard's Vindication," in *Report and Collections of the State Historical Society of Wisconsin*, 289–296; Albert Salisbury, "Green County Pioneers," in *Report and Collections of the State Historical Society of Wisconsin*, vol. 6 (Madison: State Historical Society of Wisconsin, 1872), 401–415.

37. Obituary of Wm. H. Houghton, *The Christian Standard* (Cincinnati, Ohio), April 18, 1885.

Chapter 3

1. Clifford L. Lord and Carl Ubberlohde, *Clio's Servant: The State Historical Society of Wisconsin 1846–1954* (Madison: State Historical Society of Wisconsin, 1967), 177–178, 301–302.

2. "Beouchard's Narrative," in *The History of Wisconsin in Three Parts*, 209.

3. Carver, *Travels through the Interior Parts of North America*, 46–47.

4. The soils of the site are classified as Edmund silt loam (eroded) and Sogn silt loam. See *Soil Survey of Dane County, Wisconsin*, Sheet 109 (United States Department of Agriculture Soil Conservation Service: 1978), 27, 67; Map of the Bedrock Geology of Wisconsin, Wisconsin Geological and Natural History Survey, 2005.

5. M. Catherine Bird and Paula J. Porubcan, *Phase III Data Recovery of Fort Walker (a.k.a. Beggs' Fort 11-Wi-1248): Plainfield Township, Will County, Illinois*. Cultural Resource Management Report No. 864 (Harvard, IL: Midwest Archaeological Research Services Inc., 2001); Floyd Mansberger and Christopher Stratton, "'Perfectly Panic Struck': The Archaeology of the Apple River Fort, Jo Daviess County, Illinois," (Springfield, IL: Fever River Research, 1996).

6. Wes Palmer, Andrew Pye, and Connie Rogers, "Texian Campaigne," *Transferware Collectors Club Bulletin* 9, no. 3 (Summer 2008): 8–10.

7. Esau Johnson Papers.

8. Ibid.

Chapter 4

1. Mansberger and Stratton, "Perfectly Panic Struck"; Bird and Porubcan, *Phase III Data Recovery of Fort Walker.*

2. Vicki L. Twinde-Javner, *Rediscovery of Second Fort Crawford (47Cr247): A Nineteenth Century Military Post on the Frontier of the Mississippi River 1839 to 1856.* Mississippi Valley Archaeology Center, University of Wisconsin–La Crosse, Reports of Investigations No. 570, 2005, 183.

3. Esau Johnson Papers.

4. Ebenezer Brigham to John H. Kinzie, June 16, 1832, in Whitney, *Black Hawk War,* vol. 2, part 1, 602.

5. Robert Braun, personal communication, December 6, 2011.

6. Esau Johnson Papers.

7. Carl P. Russell, *Guns on the Early Frontiers* (Berkeley: University of California Press, 1957), 151–160.

8. Crawford and Crawford, *Memoirs of Iowa County,* 25.

9. T. M. Hamilton, *Firearms on the Frontier: Guns at Fort Michilimackinac 1715–1781* (Mackinac Island, MI: Mackinac Island Park Commission, 1976), 33–35.

10. Berkeley R. Lewis, *Small Arms and Ammunition in the United States Service,* Smithsonian Institution Publication 4254, Washington, DC, 1956.

11. Twinde-Javner, *Rediscovery of Second Fort Crawford,* 100–101.

12. Crawford and Crawford, *Memoirs of Iowa County,* 25.

13. Twinde-Javner, *Rediscovery of Second Fort Crawford,* 102–106.

14. Russell, *Guns on the Early Frontiers,* 238; Twinde-Javner, *Rediscovery of Second Fort Crawford,* 106.

15. Lewis Winant, *Early Percussion Firearms* (New York: Bonanza Books, 1956).

16. Mansberger and Stratton, "Perfectly Panic Struck," 97.

17. See, for example, Edward E. Loftstrom, "An Analysis of Temporal Change in a Nineteenth Century Ceramic Assemblage from Fort Snelling, Minnesota," *The Minnesota Archaeologist* 35, no. 1 (1976): 16–40; Robert Mazrim, "'Now Quite Out of Society': Archaeology and Frontier Illinois: Essays and Excavation Reports," Illinois Transportation Archaeology Bulletin 1 (Springfield: Illinois Transportation Archaeological Research Program, Department of Anthropology, University of Illinois at Urbana–Champaign, 2002); George L. Milner, "Classification and Economic Scaling of Nineteenth Century Ceramics," *Historical Archaeology* 14 (1980): 1–40; Ivor Noël Hume, *A Guide to Artifacts of Colonial America* (New York: Alfred A. Knopf, 1978).

18. Mazrim, "Now Quite Out of Society," 278.

19. Mansberger and Stratton, "Perfectly Panic Struck," 77.

20. Arnold A. Kowalsky and Dorothy E. Kowalsky, *Encyclopedia of Marks on American, English, and European Earthenware, Ironstone, and Stoneware 1780–1980* (Atglen, PA: Schiffer Publishing Co., 1999), 85; Dick Henrywood, "Tams, Anderson & Tams—Mystery Solved," *Transferprint Collectors Club Bulletin* 11, no. 1 (Winter 2010): 12.

21. Palmer, Pye, and Rogers, "Texian Campaigne," 8–10.

22. George L. Miller and Robert R. Hunter Jr., "English Shell-Edged Earthenware: Alias Leeds Ware, Alias Feather Edge," The Consumer Revolution in 18th Century English Pottery, Proceedings of the Wedgewood International Seminar, no. 35 (Birmingham, AL: Birmingham Arts Museum, 1990): 107–136.

23. Lynne Sussman, *Mocha, Banded, Cat's Eye, and Other Factory-Made Slipware (Studies in Northeast Historical Archaeology)*, no. 1 (Boston: Boston University, 1997), 15–17.

24. John Ramsay, *American Potters and Pottery* (New York: Hale, Cushman, and Flint, 1939).

25. Mansberger and Stratton, "Perfectly Panic Struck," 88.

26. Mazrim, "Now Quite Out of Society," 40–41.

27. Juliette M. Kinzie, *Wau-Bun: The "Early Day" in the North-West* (Urbana and Chicago: University of Illinois Press, 1992), 80.

28. Ibid., 169–170, 181. Mansberger and Stratton, "Perfectly Panic Struck," 118.

29. Twinde-Javner, *Rediscovery of Second Fort Crawford*, 157–158.

30. Ibid., 169–170, 181.

31. Ibid., 174.

32. J. Byron Sudbury, "An Illustrated 1895 Catalogue of the Akron Smoking Pipe Co.," in *Historic Clay Pipe Studies* 3, ed. J. Byron Sudbury (Ponca City, OK: privately published, 1986), 1–42.

33. Twinde-Javner, *Rediscovery of Second Fort Crawford*, 165–166.

34. Lee H. Nelson, "Nail Chronology as an Aid to Dating Old Buildings," American Association for State and Local History Technical Leaflet no. 48 (1968).

35. Ebenezer Brigham Papers.

36. Plat map for T6N, R6E surveyed in 1833, Bureau of the Commissioner of Public Lands, General Land Office Records, Madison, Wisconsin.

37. Esau Johnson Papers.

38. Bird and Porubcan, *Phase III Data Recovery of Fort Walker*, 95–97.

39. Ebenezer Brigham Papers.

40. Barbara Luecke, *Feeding the Frontier Army* (Eagan, MN: Grenadier Publications, 1990), 113.

41. Essau Johnson Papers.

42. Col. James M. Rice, *Peoria City and County*, vol. 1 (Chicago: S. J. Clark Publishing, 1912), 259; Peoria County Historical Society, www.peoriahistoricalsociety.org/peohistoryamer.html; Kerry A. Trask, *Black Hawk*, 183.

43. Mansberger and Stratton, "Perfectly Panic Struck," 85–87.

Appendix I

1. President Andrew Jackson called up reinforcements from New Orleans, but an outbreak of cholera among the troops kept them in Chicago. See Trask, *Black Hawk: The Battle for the Heart of America*, 272–276.

2. John Carl Parish, *George Wallace Jones* (Iowa City: State Historical Society of Iowa, 1912), 10, 115.

3. *Portrait and Biographical Record of Dubuque, Jones and Clayton Counties, Iowa* (Salem, MA: Higginson Book Co., 1894), 151.

4. Whitney, *Black Hawk War*, vol. 2, part 1, 462; Whitney, *Black Hawk War*, vol. 2, part 2, 1227.

5. Robert Braun, *The Forts of the Michigan Territory Mineral District during the Black Hawk War* (Fort Atkinson, WI: Old Lead Mine Region Historical Society, 2000), 9, 10.

6. Smith, *The History of Wisconsin: From Exploration to Statehood*, 185.

7. George Fiedler, *Mineral Point: A History*, 2nd ed. (Madison: State Historical Society of Wisconsin, 1973), 36.

8. Crawford and Crawford, *Memoirs of Iowa County*, 24; Wisconsin Muster Rolls from the Black Hawk War, 1832, typescript of original muster rolls in the records of the General Accounting Office (Record Group 217) at the National Archives, Washington DC, www.wisconsinhistory.org/turningpoints/search.asp?id=1586.

9. Braun, *The Forts of the Michigan Territory Mineral District during the Black Hawk War*, 4–5.

10. Sylvan J. Muldoon, *Alexander Hamilton's Pioneer Son: The Life and Times of Colonel William Stephen Hamilton: 1797-1850* (Harrisburg, PA: Aurand Press, 1930); Lucile Monson Bisegger, Marjean Hartwick Bondele, and Harriet Olson Halloran, *William Stephen Hamilton's Wiota: 1828-Diggings-1993* (Gratiot, WI: L. Bisegger, 1993).

11. "Beouchard's Narrative," in *The History of Wisconsin in Three Parts*, 210.

12. Dodge's dramatic account of the battle of can be found in his communication to Henry Atkinson, dated June 18, 1832, in Whitney, *Black Hawk War*, vol. 2, part 1, 622–625.

13. Ibid., 625.

14. Mansberger and Stratton, "Perfectly Panic Struck," 6–9.

15. Jackson, *Black Hawk: An Autobiography*, 128.

16. Ibid., 129–131. In his autobiography, Black Hawk refers variously to one medicine bag or several. Dogs were killed and eaten for special occasions. As was the case before the attack on the Apple River Fort, dog feasts were held before raids, with the leader of the raid preparing the feast. When Stillman's militia assaulted Black Hawk's band, however, Black Hawk was holding a dog feast for the Potawatomi, to whom he was making a request for food (*Black Hawk: An Autobiography*, 122).

17. Mansberger and Stratton, "Perfectly Panic Struck," 6–9.

18. Mansberger and Stratton, "Perfectly Panic Struck."

❧ BIBLIOGRAPHY ❧

Beggs, S. R. *Pages from the Early History of the West and North-West*. Cincinnati: R P. Thompson, 1868.

Beouchard, Edward. "Beouchard's Narrative." In *The History of Wisconsin in Three Parts, Historical, Documentary, and Descriptive*, ed. William Smith, part 2. Madison: B. Brown, 1854, 209–214.

———. "Beouchard's Vindication." In *Report and Collections of the State Historical Society of Wisconsin*, vol. 7. Madison: State Historical Society of Wisconsin, 1876, 289–296.

Bird, M. Catherine, and Paula J. Porubcan. *Phase III Data Recovery of Fort Walker (a.k.a. Beggs' Fort 11-Wi-1248): Plainfield Township, Will County, Illinois*. Cultural Resource Management Report No. 864. Harvard, IL: Midwest Archaeological Research Services Inc., 2001.

Bisegger, Lucile Monson, Marjean Hartwick Bondele, and Harriet Olson Halloran. *William Stephen Hamilton's Wiota: 1828-Diggings-1993*. Gratiot, WI: L. Bisegger, 1993.

Braun, Robert. *The Forts of the Michigan Territory Mineral District during the Black Hawk War*. Fort Atkinson, WI: Old Lead Mine Area Historical Society, 2000.

Brigham, Ebenezer, Papers, 1816–1887. Wisconsin Historical Society Archives, Madison, WI.

Brown, Mark M. *The Flight of the Nez Perce*. Lincoln: University of Nebraska Press, 1982.

Bureau of the Commissioner of Public Lands, General Land Office Records, Madison, Wisconsin.

Carver, Jonathan. *Travels through the Interior Parts of North America, in the Years 1766, 1767, and 1768.* Minneapolis: Ross and Haines, 1965.

Chapman, Charles C. *History of Fulton County, Illinois.* Peoria: Charles C. Chapman and Co., 1879.

Chapman Publishing Company. *Portrait and Biographical Record of Dubuque, Jones and Clayton Counties, Iowa: Containing Biographical Sketches of Prominent and Representative Citizens of the Counties, Together with Biographies and Portraits of All the Presidents of the United States.* Chicago: Chapman Pub. Co., 1894.

Crawford, George M., and Robert Crawford, eds. *Memoirs of Iowa County: From the Earliest Historical Times Down to the Present.* Chicago: Northwestern Historical Association, 1913.

Drake, Benjamin Drake. *Life of Tecumseh and of His Brother the Prophet; With a Historical Sketch of the Shawanoe Indians.* Mount Vernon: Rose Press, 2008.

Fiedler, George. *Mineral Point: A History,* 2nd ed. Madison: State Historical Society of Wisconsin, 1973.

Hall, John W. *Uncommon Defense: Indian Allies in the Black Hawk War.* Cambridge, MA: Harvard University Press, 2009.

Hamilton, T. M. *Firearms on the Frontier: Guns at Fort Michilimackinac 1715–1781.* Mackinac Island, MI: Mackinac Island Park Commission, 1976.

Henrywood, Dick. "Tams, Anderson & Tams—Mystery Solved." *Transferprint Collectors Club Bulletin* 11, no. 1 (winter 2010): 12–13.

Hume, Ivor Noël. *A Guide to Artifacts of Colonial America.* New York: Alfred A. Knopf, 1978.

Jackson, Donald, ed. *Black Hawk: An Autobiography.* Urbana: University of Illinois Press, 1964.

Johnson, Esau, Papers, 1800–1882. Wisconsin Historical Society Archives, Madison, WI.

Jung, Patrick J. "The Black Hawk War Reconsidered: A New Interpretation of its Causes and Consequences." *Journal of the Indian Wars* 1, no. 2 (1999): 30–69.

———. *The Black Hawk War of 1832.* Norman: University of Oklahoma Press, 2007.

Kinzie, Juliette M. *Wau-Bun: The "Early Day" in the North-West.* Urbana and Chicago: University of Illinois Press, 1992.

Kehoe, Alice Beck. *The Ghost Dance: Ethnohistory and Revitalization*, 2nd ed. Long Grove, IL: Waveland Press, 2006.

Kowalsky, Arnold, and Dorothy E. Kowalsky. *Encyclopedia of Marks on American, English, and European Earthenware, Ironstone, and Stoneware 1780–1980*. Atglen, PA: Schiffer Publishing Co., 1999.

Lewis, Berkeley R. *Small Arms and Ammunition in the United States Service*. Washington, DC: Smithsonian Institution Publication 4254 (1956).

Loftstrom, Edward E. "An Analysis of Temporal Change in a Nineteenth Century Ceramic Assemblage from Fort Snelling, Minnesota." *The Minnesota Archaeologist* 35, no. 1 (1976): 16–40.

Lord, Clifford L., and Carl Ubberlohde. *Clio's Servant: The State Historical Society of Wisconsin 1846–1954*. Madison: State Historical Society of Wisconsin, 1967.

Luecke, Barbara. *Feeding the Frontier Army*. Eagan, MN: Grenadier Publications, 1990.

Mansberger, Floyd, and Christopher Stratton. "'Perfectly Panic Struck': The Archaeology of the Apple River Fort, Jo Daviess County, Illinois." Springfield, IL: Fever River Research, 1996.

Mazrim, Robert. "'Now Quite Out of Society': Archaeology and Frontier Illinois: Essays and Excavation Reports." Illinois Transportation Archaeology Bulletin 1 (Springfield: Illinois Transportation Archaeological Research Program, Department of Anthropology, University of Illinois at Urbana–Champaign, 2002).

Miller, George L., and Robert R. Hunter Jr. "English Shell-Edged Earthenware: Alias Leeds Ware, Alias Feather Edge." The Consumer Revolution in 18th Century English Pottery, Proceedings of the Wedgewood International Seminar, no. 35 (Birmingham, AL: Birmingham Arts Museum, 1990): 107–136.

Milner, George L. "Classification and Economic Scaling of Nineteenth Century Ceramics." *Historical Archaeology* 14 (1980): 1–40.

Muldoon, Sylvan J. *Alexander Hamilton's Pioneer Son: The Life and Times of Colonel William Stephen Hamilton: 1797–1850*. Harrisburg, PA: Aurand Press, 1930.

Nelson, Lee H. "Nail Chronology as an Aid to Dating Old Buildings." American Association for State and Local History Technical Leaflet no. 48 (1968).

Nichols, Roger L. *Black Hawk and the Warrior's Path*. Arlington Heights, IL: Harlan Davidson, 1992.

———. "The Black Hawk War in Retrospect," *Wisconsin Magazine of History* 65, no. 4 (Summer 1982): 239–246.

Obituary of Wm. H. Houghton. *The Christian Standard* (Cincinnati, Ohio). April 18, 1885.

Palmer, Wes, Andrew Pye, and Connie Rogers. "Texian Campaigne." *Transferware Collectors Club Bulletin* 9, no. 3 (Summer 2008): 8–10.

Patterson, John B., ed. *Life of Ma-ka-tai-me-she-kia-kiak or Black Hawk*. St. Louis, 1882.

Portrait and Biographical Record of Dubuque, Jones and Clayton Counties, Iowa. Salem, MA: Higginson Book Co., 1894.

Ramsay, John. *American Potters and Pottery*. New York: Hale, Cushman, and Flint, 1939.

Russell, Carl P. *Guns on the Early Frontiers*. Berkeley: University of California Press, 1957.

Smith, Alice E. *The History of Wisconsin: Exploration to Statehood*, vol. 1. Madison: State Historical Society of Wisconsin, 1973.

Sudbury, J. Byron, ed. *Historic Clay Pipe Studies* 3. Ponca City, OK: Privately Published, 1986.

Sugden, John. *Tecumseh: A Life*. New York: Holt Paperbacks, 1997.

Sussman, Lynne. *Mocha, Banded, Cat's Eye, and Other Factory-Made Slipware (Studies in Northeast Historical Archaeology)*, no. 1. Boston: Boston University, 1997.

Taylor, Richard C. "Notes Respecting Certain Indian Mounds and Earthworks in the Form of Animal Effigies, Chiefly in Wisconsin Territory, U.S." *American Journal of Science and Art* 34 (1838): 88–104.

Tenney, H. A. "Early Times in Wisconsin." In *First Annual Report and Collections of the State Historical Society of Wisconsin*, vol. 1. Madison: State Historical Society of Wisconsin, 1855.

Trask, Kerry A. *Black Hawk: The Battle for the Heart of America*. New York: Henry Holt and Company, 2007.

Twinde-Javner, Vicki L. *Rediscovery of Second Fort Crawford (47Cr247): A Nineteenth Century Military Post on the Frontier of the Mississippi River 1839 to 1856*. Mississippi Valley Archaeology Center, University of Wisconsin–La Crosse, Reports of Investigations No. 570, 2005.

United States Department of Agriculture. *Soil Survey of Dane County, Wisconsin*. United States Department of Agriculture in Cooperation with the Research Division of the Agricultural and Life Sciences, University of Wisconsin, 1978.

Wallace, Anthony F. C. "Prelude to Disaster: The Course of Indian-White Relations Which Led to the Black Hawk War of 1832." In *The Black Hawk*

War, 1831–1832, comp. and ed. Ellen M. Whitney, vol. 1, part 1. Springfield, IL: Illinois State Historical Library, 1970.

Whitney, Ellen M., comp. and ed. *The Black Hawk War, 1831–1832*. 3 vols. Springfield, IL: Illinois State Historical Library, 1970–1975.

Winant, Lewis. *Early Percussion Firearms*. New York: Bonanza Books, 1956.

Wisconsin Geological and Natural History Survey. Map of the Bedrock Geology of Wisconsin, 2005.

Wisconsin Muster Rolls from the Black Hawk War, 1832. Typescript of original muster rolls in the records of the General Accounting Office (Record Group 217) at the National Archives, Washington, DC, www.wisconsinhistory.org/turningpoints/search.asp?id=1586.

Appendix II: Sources Cited

Andreas, Alfred T. *History of Cook County Illinois from Earliest Period to the Present Time*. Chicago: Alfred T. Andreas, 1884.

Bateman, Newton, and Paul Selby. *Historical Encyclopedia of Illinois and the History of Warren County*. Chicago: Munsell Publishing Company, 1903.

Beers, J. H., and Company. *Commemorative Biographical Record of the Counties of Rock, Green, Grant, Iowa and Lafayette, Wisconsin*. Chicago: J. H. Beers and Company, 1901.

Beggs, S. R. *Pages from the Early History of the West and North-West*. Cincinnati: R. P. Thompson, 1868.

Bird, M. Catherine, and Paula J. Porubcan. *Phase III Data Recovery of Fort Walker (a.k.a. Beggs' Fort 11-Wi-1248): Plainfield Township, Will County, Illinois*. Cultural Resource Management Report No. 864. Harvard, IL: Midwest Archaeological Research Services Inc., 2001.

Bisegger, Lucile Monson, Marjean Hartwick Bondele, and Harriet Olson Halloran. *William Stephen Hamilton's Wiota: 1828-Diggings-1993*. Gratiot, WI: D. L. Johnson, 1993.

Blanchard, Rufus. *The History of DuPage County, Illinois*. Chicago: O. L. Baskin and Company, 1882.

Bowen, Alice. *The Story of Savanna: The First Hundred Years (1928)*. genealogytrails.com/ill/carroll/savanna100.html.

Braun, Robert. *The Forts of the Michigan Territory Mineral District during the Black Hawk War*. Fort Atkinson, WI: Old Lead Mine Region Historical Society, 2000.

Butterfield, C. W. *History of Elkhart County, Indiana*. Chicago: Charles C. Chapman and Co., 1881.

———. *History of Fulton County, Illinois.* Peoria: Charles C. Chapman and Co., 1879.

———. *History of Grant County, Wisconsin.* Chicago: Western Historical Company, 1881.

———. *History of Iowa County, Wisconsin.* Chicago: Western Historical Company, 1881.

History of Lafayette County, Wisconsin. Chicago: Western Historical Company, 1881. Reprinted by the Lafayette County Historical Society, 1983.

Chapman, Charles C., and Co. *History of Knox County, Illinois.* Peoria: Charles C. Chapman and Co., 1878.

———. *History of Tazewell County, Illinois.* Chicago: C. Chapman and Co., 1879.

Crawford, George M., and Robert Crawford, eds. *Memoirs of Iowa County: From the Earliest Historical Times Down to the Present.* Chicago: Northwestern Historical Association, 1913.

Ellsworth, Spencer. *Records of the Olden Time, or, Fifty Years on the Prairies: Embracing Sketches of the Discovery, Exploration and Settlement of the Country, the Organization of the Counties of Putnam and Marshall, Incidents and Reminiscences Connected therewith, Biographies of Citizens, Portraits and Illustrations.* Lacon, IL: Home Journal Printing Establishment, 1880.

Fieldler, George. *Mineral Point: A History*, 2nd ed. Madison: State Historical Society of Wisconsin, 1973.

Ford, Henry A. *Earliest Historical Facts of Marshall-Putnam Counties Also Bureau and Stark Counties Embracing an Account of the Settlement and Early Progress.* Lacon, IL: Henry A. Ford, 1960.

Goodspeed, Weston A. "Greenfield Township." In *Counties of La Grange and Noble, Indiana: Historical and Biographical,* by J. H. Herrick, John Paul Jones, Weston A. Goodspeed, and R. H. Herrick. Chicago: F. A. Battey and Co., 1882.

Gregg, Thomas. *History of Hancock County, Illinois.* Chicago: Chas C. Chapman and Co., 1880.

Halsey, John R. "Fort Hogan: Michigan's One-Day Black Hawk War Stockade." *Michigan Magazine of History* 75, no. 2 (1991): 10.

Hasbrouck, Jacob L. *History of McLean County, Illinois.* Topeka, KS: Historical Publishing Co., 1924.

Hoffman, U. L. *History of LaSalle County.* Chicago: S. J. Clark and Co., 1906.

Holford, Castello N. *History of Grant County, Wisconsin: Including its Civil, Political, Geological, Mineralogical, Archaeological and Military History, and a History of the Several Towns.* Lancaster, WI: The Teller Print, 1900.

Howard, Robert P. *Illinois: A History of the Prairie State*. Grand Rapids, MI: William B. Eermans Publishing Co., 1972.

Jones, George W. "Impromptu Speech of George W. Jones." In *Report of the Organization and First Reunion of the Tri-State Old Settlers*. Keokuk, IA: Tri-State Printing Co., 1884.

Jung, Patrick J. *The Black Hawk War of 1832*. Norman: University of Oklahoma Press, 2007.

Kett, H. F., and Co. *History of Carroll County, Illinois*. Chicago: H. F. Kett and Co., 1878.

———. *The Past and Present of Warren County, Illinois*. Chicago: H. F. Kett and Co., 1877.

Lake City Publishing Co. *Portrait and Biological Record of Hancock, McDonough and Henderson Counties, Illinois*. Chicago: Lake City Publishing Co., 1894.

Leonard, Doris Parr. *Big and Bright Prairies: A History of Bureau County, Illinois*. Moline, IL: Desauliers and Company, 1968.

Loftus, Carrie. *Indiana Militia in the Black Hawk War*. Signal Mountain, TN: Mountain Press, 2003.

Mansberger, Floyd, and Christopher Stratton. "'Perfectly Panic Struck': The Archaeology of the Apple River Fort, Jo Daviess County, Illinois." Springfield, IL: Fever River Research, 1996.

Maune, August. *History of Will County, Illinois*. Topeka and Indianapolis: Historical Publishing County, 1928.

Parish, John Carl. *George Wallace Jones*. Iowa City: State Historical Society of Iowa, 1912.

Pioneer Society of the State of Michigan. *Pioneer Collections, Report of the Pioneer Society of the State of Michigan*, vol. 2. Detroit: Wm. Graham's Presses, 1880.

Rasmusen, Marilyn. *LaSalle County Lore*. Henry, IL: M and D Printing Company Inc., 1992.

Salisbury, Albert. "Green County Pioneers." In *Report and Collections of the State Historical Society of Wisconsin*, vol. 6. Madison: State Historical Society of Wisconsin, 1872, 401–415.

Slane, Odillion B. *Reminiscences of Early Peoria, Including Indian Stories*. Peoria, IL: Privately Printed, 1933.

Stanfield, Judge Thomas S. *The Black Hawk War*. In *History of St. Joseph County Indiana*. Chicago: Charles C. Chapman and Co., 1880.

Watson, Elmo Scott. "Henline Stockade, Lawndale, Township McLean Township." *Ancestors Yours and Mine*, vol. 1, no. 3. Lexington, IL: Lexington Genealogical and Historical Society, 1975.

Whitney, Ellen M., comp. and ed. *The Black Hawk War, 1831–1832*. 3 vols. Springfield, IL: Illinois State Historical Library, 1970–1975.

Wilgus, James A. "History of Old Platteville: 1827–1835." *Wisconsin Magazine of History* 28, no. 1 (1944): 48–80.

Wilson, William, and Kevin Kaegy. *Forts and Blockhouses of Early Illinois.* Bloomington, IN: Tafford Publishing, 2006.

Wisconsin Muster Rolls from the Black Hawk War, 1832. Typescript of original muster rolls in the records of the General Accounting Office (Record Group 217) at the National Archives, Washington, DC, www.wisconsinhistory.org/turningpoints/search.asp?id=1586.

Woodruff, George H. *History of Will County, Illinois.* Chicago: Wm. Le Baron Jr. & Company, 1878.

≈ INDEX ≈

Photos and illustrations are indicated by page numbers in bold text.